M000307725

POETRY FROM CRESCENT MOON

William Shakespeare: *The Sonnets*
edited, with an introduction by Mark Tuley

William Shakespeare: *Complete Poems*
edited and introduced by Mark Tuley

Edmund Spenser: *Heavenly Love: Selected Poems*
selected and introduced by Teresa Page

Edmund Spenser: *Amoretti*
edited by Teresa Page

Robert Herrick: *Delight In Disorder: Selected Poems*
edited and introduced by M.K. Pace

Sir Thomas Wyatt: *Love For Love: Selected Poems*
selected and introduced by Louise Cooper

John Donne: *Air and Angels: Selected Poems*
selected and introduced by A.H. Ninham

D.H. Lawrence: *Being Alive: Selected Poems*
edited with an introduction by Margaret Elvy

D.H. Lawrence: Symbolic Landscapes
by Jane Foster

D.H. Lawrence: Infinite Sensual Violence
by M.K. Pace

Percy Bysshe Shelley: *Paradise of Golden Lights: Selected Poems*
selected and introduced by Charlotte Greene

Thomas Hardy: *Her Haunting Ground: Selected Poems*
edited, with an introduction by A.H. Ninham

Sexing Hardy: Thomas Hardy and Feminism
by Margaret Elvy

Emily Bronte: *Darkness and Glory: Selected Poems*
selected and introduced by Miriam Chalk

John Keats: *Bright Star: Selected Poems*
edited with an introduction by Miriam Chalk

Rainer Maria Rilke: *Dance the Orange:* Selected Poems
translated by Michael Hamburger

German Romantic Poetry: Goethe, Novalis, Heine, Hölderlin
by Carol Appleby

Arseny Tarkovsky: *Life, Life: Selected Poems*
translated by Virginia Rounding

Emily Dickinson: *Wild Nights: Selected Poems*
selected and introduced by Miriam Chalk

Diana
by Henry Constable

Delia
by Samuel Daniel

Idea
by Michael Drayton

Astrophil and Stella
by Sir Philip Sidney

Elizabethan Sonnet Cycles
by Daniel, Drayton, Sidney, Spenser and Shakespeare

Three Metaphysical Poets

Selected Poems

Three Metaphysical Poets
Selected Poems

John Donne
Robert Herrick
Henry Vaughan

Edited by A.H. Ninham

CRESCENT MOON

Crescent Moon Publishing
P.O. Box 1312
Maidstone, Kent
ME14 5XU, U.K.
www.crmoon.com

First published 2016.
Introductions © A.H. Ninham and M.K. Pace, 1994, 2008, 2016.

Printed and bound in the U.S.A..
Set in Garamond Book 12 on 15pt.
Designed by Radiance Graphics.

The right of A.H. Ninham to be identified as the editor of *Three Metaphysical Poets* has been asserted generally in accordance with sections 77 and 78 of the Copyright, Designs and Patents Act 1988.

British Library Cataloguing in Publication data

ISBN-13 9781861715449

Contents

ROBERT HERRICK

HENRY VAUGHAN

Only a little more
  I have to write,
   Then I'll give o're,
And bid the world Goodnight.

Robert Herrick, from 'His Poetrie His Pillar'

John Donne

Robert Herrick

Henry Vaughan

JOHN DONNE

Song: Go and Catch a Falling Star

Go and catch a falling star,
  Get with child a mandrake root,
Tell me, where all past years are,
  Or who cleft the devil's foot,
Teach me to hear mermaids singing,
  Or to keep off envy's stinging,
        And find
        What wind
Serves to advance an honest mind.

If thou born to strange sights,
  Things invisible to see,
Ride ten thousand days and nights,
  Till age snow white hairs on thee,
Thou, when thou return'st, wilt tell me
All strange wonders that befell thee,
        And swear
        No where
Lives a woman true, and fair.

If thou find'st one, let me know,
  Such a pilgrimage were sweet,
Yet do not, I would not go,
  Though at next door we might meet,
Though she were true, when you met her,
And last, till you write your letter,
        Yet she

23

Will be
False, ere I come, to two, or three.

The Primose

Upon this primrose hill,
Where, if heaven would distil
A shower of rain, each several drop might go
To his own primrose, and grow man so;
And where their form, and their infinity
Make a terrestrial galaxy,
As the small stars do in the sky:
I walk to find a true love; and I see
That 'tis not a mere woman, that is she,
But must, or more, or less than woman be.

Yet know I not, which flower
I wish; a six, or four;
For should my true love less than woman be,
She were scarce anything; and then, should she
Be more than woman, she would get above
All thought of sex, and think to move
My heart to study her, not to love;
Both these were monsters; since there must
reside
Falsehood in woman, I could more abide,
She were by art, than nature falsified.

Live primroses then, and thrive
With thy true number, five;
And women, whom this flower doth represent,
With this mysterious number be content;
Ten is the farthest number; if half ten

Belong unto each woman, then
Each woman may take half us men;
Or if this will not serve their turn, since all
Numbers are odd, or even, and they fall
First into this, five, women may take us all.

Love's Alchemy

Some that have deeper digged love's mine than I,
Say, where his centric happiness doth lie:
        I have loved, and got, and told,
But should I love, get, tell, till I were old,
I should not find that hidden mystery;
        Oh, 'tis impostur all:
And as no chemic yet the elixir got,
        But glorifies his pregnant pot,
        If by the way to him befall
Some odoriferous thing, or medicinal,
    So, lovers dreams a rich and long delight,
    But get a winter-seeming summer's night.

Our ease, our thrift, our honour, and our day,
Shall we, for this vain bubble's shadow pay?
        Ends love in this, that my man,
Can be as happy as I can; if he can
Endure the short scorn of a bridegroom's play?
        That loving wretch that swears,
'Tis not the bodies marry, but her angelic finds,
        Would swear as justly, that he hears,
In that day's rude hoarse minstrelsy, the spheres.
Hope not for mind in women; at their best
    Sweetness and wit, they are but mummy,
                                    possessed.

Air and Angels

Twice or thrice had I loved thee,
Before I knew thy face or name;
So in a voice, so in a shapeless flame,
Angels affect us oft, and worshipped be;
   Still, when, to where thou wert, I came,
Some lovely glorious nothing I did see,
   But since my soul, whose child love is,
Takes limbs of flesh, and else could nothing do,
   More subtle than the parent is
Love must not be, but take a body too,
   And therefore what thou wert, and who
      I bid love ask, and now
That it assume thy body, I allow,
And fix itself in thy lip, eye, and brow.

Whilst thus to ballast love, I thought,
And so more steadily to have gone,
With waves which would sink admiration,
I saw, I had love's pinnace overfraught,
   Every thy hair for love to work upon
Is much too much, some fitter must be sought;
   For, nor in nothing, nor in things
Extreme, and scatt'rings bright, can love in here;
   Then as an angel, face and wings
Of air, not pure as it, yet pure doth wear,
   So thy love may be my love's sphere;
      Just such disparity

As is 'twixt air and angels' purity,
'Twixt women's love, and men's will ever be.

The Extasie

Where, like a pillow on a bed,
　A pregnant bank swelled up, to rest
The violet's reclining head,
　Sat we two, one another's best;

Our hands were firmly cemented
　With a false balm, which thence did spring,
Our eye-beams twisted, and did thread
　Our eyes, upon one double string;

So to' intergraft our hands, as yet
　Was all our means to make us one,
And pictures in our eyes to get
　Was all our propagation.

As 'twixt two equal armies, Fate
　Suspends uncertain victory,
Our souls, (which to advance their state,
　Were gone), hung 'twixt her, and me.

And whilst our souls negotiate there,
　We like sepulchral statues lay;
All day, the same our postures were,
　And we said nothing, all the day.

If any, so by love refined,
　That he soul's language understood,
And by god love were grown all mind,

Within convenient distance stood,

He (though he knew not which soul spake
  Because both meant, both spake the same)
Might thence a new concoction take,
  And part far purer than he came.

This extasie doth unperplex
  (We said) and tell us what we love,
We see by this, it was not sex,
  We see, we saw not what did move:

But as all several souls contain
  Mixture of things, they know not what,
Love, these mixed souls doth mix again,
  And makes both one, each this and that.

A single violet transplant,
  The strength, the colour, and the size,
(All which before was poor, and scant,)
  Redoubles still, and multiplies.

When love, with one another so
  Interinanimates two souls,
That abler soul, which thence doth flow,
  Defects of loneliness controls.

We then, who are this new soul, know,
  Of what we are composed, and made,
For, th' atomies of which we grow,
  Are souls, whom no change can invade.

But O alas, so long, so far
    Our bodies why do we forbear?
They are ours, though they are not we, we are
    The intelligences, they the sphere.

We owe them thanks, because they thus,
    Did us, at first convey,
Yielded their forces, sense, to us,
    Nor are dross to us, but allay.

On man heaven's influences works not so,
    But that it first imprints the air,
So soul into the soul may flow,
    Though it to body first repair.

As our blood labours to beget
    Spirits, as like souls as it can,
Because such fingers need to knit
    That subtle knot, which makes us man:

So must pure lovers' souls descend
    T' affections, and to faculties,
Which sense may reach and apprehend,
    Else a great prince in prison lies.

To our bodies turn we then, that so
    Weak men on love revealed may look;
Love's mysteries in souls do grow,
    But yet the body is his book.

And if some lover, such as we,
    Have heard this dialogue of one,

Let him still mark us, he shall see
   Small change, when we' are to bodies gone.

from The Relic

First, we loved well and faithfully,
Yet knew not what we loved, nor why,
Difference of sex no more we knew,
Than our guardian angels do;
Coming and going, we
Perchance might kiss, but not between those meals;
Our hands ne'er touched the seals,
Which nature, injured by late law, sets free:
These miracles we did; but now alas,
All measure, and all language, I should pass,
Should I tell what a miracle she was.

from The Prohibition

Yet, love and hate me too,
So, these extremes shall neither's office do;
Love me, that I may die the gentler way;
Hate me, because thy love's too great for me;
Or let these two, themselves, not me decay;
So shall I live thy stage, nor triumph be;
Lest thou my love and hate and me undo,
To let me live, Oh love and hate me too.

from The Canonization

Call us what you will, we are made such by love;
  Call her one, me another fly,
We are tapers too, and at our own cost die,
  And we in us find the eagle and the dove,
    The phoenix riddle hath more wit
    By us; we two being one, are it.
So to one neutral thing both sexes fit
  We die and rise the same, and prove
  Mysterious by this love.

Break of Day

'Tis true, 'tis day, what though it be?
O wilt thou therefore rise from me?
Why should we rise, because 'tis light?
Did we lie down, because 'twas night?
Love which in spite of darkness brought us hither,
Should in despite of light keep us together.

Light hath no tongue, but is all eye;
If it could speak as well as spy,
This were the worst, that it could say,
That being well, I fain would stay,
And that I loved my heart and honour so,
That I would not from him, that had them, go.

Must business thee from hence remove?
Oh, that's the worst disease of love,
The poor, the foul, the false, love can
Admit but not the busied man.
He which hath business, and makes love, doth do
Such wrong, as when a married man doth won.

The Bait

Come live with me, and be my love,
And we will some new pleasures prove
Of golden sands, and crystal brooks,
With silken lines, and silver hooks.

There will the river whispering run
Warmed by thy eyes, more than the sun.
And there the' enamoured fish will stay,
Begging themselves they may betray.

When thou wilt swim in that live bath,
Each fish, which every channel hath,
Will amorously to thee swim,
Gladder to catch thee, than thou him.

If thou, to be so seen, be'st loth,
By sun, or moon, thou darkenest both,
And if myself have leave to see,
I need not their light, having thee.

Lets others freeze with angling reeds,
And cut their legs, with shells and weeds,
Or treacherously poor fish beset,
With strangling snare, or windowy net:

Let coarse bold hands, from slimy nest
The bedded fish in banks out-wrest,
Or curious traitors, sleavesilk flies

*38

Bewitch poor fishes' wandering eyes.

For thee, thou need'st no such deceit,
For thou thyself art thine own bait,
That fish, that is not catched thereby,
Alas, is wiser far than I.

Song: *Sweetest Love, I Do Not Go*

Sweetest love, I do not go,
　For weariness of thee,
Nor in hope the world can show
　A fitter love for me;
　　But since that I
Must die at last, 'tis best,
To use my self in jest
　Thus by feigned deaths to die.

Yesternight the sun went hence,
　And yet is here today,
He hath no desire nor sense,
　Nor half so short a way:
　　Then fear not me,
But believe that I shall make
Speedier journeys, since I take
　More wings and spurs than he.

O how feeble is man's power,
　That if good fortune fall,
Cannot add another hour,
　Nor a lost hour recall!
　　But come bad chance,
And we join to it our strength,
And we teach it art and length,
　Itself o'er us to advance.

When thou sigh'st, thou sigh'st not wind,

But sigh'st my soul away,
When thou weep'st, unkindly kind,
  My life's blood doth decay.
    It cannot be
That thou lov'st me, as thou say'st,
If in thine my life thou waste,
  Thou art the best of me.

Let not thy diving heart
  Forethink me any ill,
Destiny may take thy part,
  And may thy fears fulfil;
    But think that we
Are but turned aside to sleep;
They who one another keep
Alive, n'er parted be.

The Dissolution

She is dead; and all which die
   To their first elements resolve;
And we were mutual elements to us,
    And made of one another.
   My body then doth hers involve,
And those things whereof I consist, hereby
In me abundant grow, and burdenous,
    And nourish not, but smother.
   My fire of passion, sighs of air,
Water of tears, and earthy sad despair,
     Which my materials be,
But near worn out by love's security,
She, to my loss, doth by her death repair,
   And I might live long wretched so
But that my fire doth with my fuel grow.
    Now as those active kings
   Whose foreign conquest treasure brings,
Receive more, and spend more, and soonest break:
This (which I amazed that I can speak)
    This death, hath with my store
     My use increased.
And so my soul more earnestly released,
Will outstrip hers; as bullets flown before
A latter bullet may o'ertake, the powder being more.

Negative Love

I never stooped so low, as they
Which on an eye, cheek, lip, can prey,
 Seldom to them, which soar no higher
 Than virtue or the mind to admire,
For sense, and understanding may
 Know, what gives fuel to their fire:
My love, though silly, is more brave,
For may I miss, whene'er I crave,
If I know yet what I would have,.

If that be simply perfectest
Which can by no way be expressed
 But negatives, my love is so.
 To all, which all love, I say no.
If any who decipher best,
 What we know not, ourselves, can know,
Let him teach me that nothing; this
As yet my ease, and comfort is,
Though I speed not, I cannot miss.

Elegy: To His Mistress Going To Bed

Come, Madam, come, all rest my powers defie,
 Until I labour, I in labour lie.
The foe oft-times having the foe in sight,
Is tir'd with standing though he never fight.

Off with that girdle, like heavens Zone glittering,
But a far fairer world incompassing.
Unpin that spangled breastplate which you wear,
That th'eyes of busie fooles may be stopt there.
Unlace your self, for that harmonious chyme,

Tells me from you, that now it is bed time.
Off with that happy busk, which I envie,
That still can be, and still can stand so nigh.
Your gown going off, such beautious state reveals,
As when from flowry meads th'hills shadow steales.

Off with that wyerie Coronet and shew
The haiery Diademe which on you doth grow:
Now off with those shooes, and then safely tread
In this loves hallow'd temple, this soft bed.
In such white robes, heaven's Angels us'd to be

Receavd by men; Thou Angel bringst with thee
A heaven like Mahomets Paradise; and though
Ill spirits walk in white, we easly know,
By this these Angels from an evil sprite,
Those set our hairs, but these our flesh upright.

* 44

Licence my roaving hands, and let them go,
Before, behind, between, above, below.
O my America! my new-found-land,
My kingdome, safliest when with one man man'd,
My Myne of precious stones, My Emperie,

How blest am I in this discovering thee!
To enter in these bonds, is to be free;
Then where my hand is set, my seal shall be.
Full nakedness! All joyes are due to thee,
As souls unbodied, bodies uncloth'd must be,

To taste whole joyes. Gems which you women use
Are like Atlanta's balls, cast in mens views,
That when a fools eye lighteth on a Gem,
His earthly soul may covet theirs, not them.
Like pictures, or like books gay coverings made

For lay-men, are all women thus array'd;
Themselves are mystick books, which only wee
(Whom their imputed grace will dignifie)
Must see reveal'd. Then since that I may know;
As liberally, as to a Midwife, shew

Thy self: cast all, yea, this white lynnen hence,
There is no pennance due to innocence.
To teach thee, I am naked first; why than
What needst thou have more covering then a man.

from Ecologue 1618. December 26

The Benediction

Blessed pair of swans, oh may you interbring
    Daily new joys, and never sing,
    Live, till all grounds of wishes fail,
Til honour, yea till wisdom grow so stale,
    That, new great heights to try,
It must serve your ambition, to die;
Raise heirs, and may here, to the world's end, live
Heirs from this King, to take thanks, yours, to give,
Nature and grace do all, and nothing art,
Ay never age, or error overthwart
With any west, these radiant eyes, with any
           north, this heart.

Epigrams

HERO AND LEANDER

Both robbed of Air, we both lie in ground,
Both whom one fire had burnt, one water drowned.

MANLINESS

Thou call'st me effeminate, for I love women's joys;
I call not thee manly, though thou follow boys.

To Mr C.B.

Thy friend, whom thy deserts to thee enchain,
  Urged by this inexcusable occasion,
  Thee and the saint of his affection
Leaving behind, doth of both wants complain;
And let the love I bear to both sustain
  No blot nor maim by this division,
Strong is this love which ties our hearts in one,
And strong that love pursued with amorous pain;
But though besides thyself I leave behind
  Heaven's liberal, and earth's thrice-fairer sun,
  Going to where stern winter aye doth won,
Yet, love's hot fires, which martyr my sad mind,
  Do send forth scalding sighs, which have the art
  To melt all ice, but that which walls her heart.

The Sun Rising

Busie old foole, unruly Sunne,
  Why dost thou thus,
Through windowes, and through curtaines call on us?
Must to thy motions lovers seasons run?
  Sawcy pedantique wretch, goe chide
  Late schoole boyes, and sowre prentices,
 Goe tell Court-huntsmen, that the King will ride,
 Call countrey ants to harvest offices;
Love, all alike, no season knowes, nor clyme,
Nor houres, dayes, moneths, which are the rags of time.

Thy beames, so reverend, and strong
  Why shouldst thou thinke?
I could eclipse and cloud them with a winke,
But that I would not lose her sight so long:
  If her eyes have not blinded thine,
  Looke, and to morrow late, tell mee,
 Whether both the'India's of spice and Myne
 Be where thou leftst them, or lie here with mee.
Aske for those Kings whom thou saw'st yesterday,
And thou shalt heare, All here in one bed lay.

She'is all States, and all Princes, I,
  Nothing else is.
Princes doe but play us; compar'd to this,
All honor's mimique; All wealth alchimie.
  Thou sunne art halfe as happy'as wee,
  In that the world's contracted thus;

Thine age askes ease, and since thy duties bee
To warme the world, that's done in warming us.
Shine here to us, and thou art every where;
This bed thy center is, these walls, thy spheare.

The Indifferent

I can love both faire and browne,
 Her whom abundance melts, and her whom want
                                    betraies,
Her who loves lonenesse best, and her who maskes and
                                    plaies,
Her whom the country form'd, and whom the town,
Her who beleeves, and her who tries,
Her who still weepes with spungie eyes,
And her who is dry corke, and never cries;
I can love her, and her, and you and you,
I can love any, so she be not true.

Will no other vice content you?
Wil it not serve your turn to do, as did your mothers?
Or have you all old vices spent, and now would finde
                                    out others?
Or doth a feare, that men are true, torment you?
Oh we are not, be not you so,
Let mee, and doe you, twenty know.
Rob mee, but binde me not, and let me goe.
Must I, who came to travaile thorow you,
Grow your fixt subject, because you are true?

Venus heard me sigh this song,
And by Loves sweetest Part, Variety, she swore,
She heard not this till now; and that it should be so no
                                    more.
She went, examin'd, and return'd ere long,

And said, alas, Some two or three
Poore Heretiques in love there bee,
Which thinke to stablish dangerous constancie.
But I have told them, since you will be true,
You shall be true to them, who'are false to you.

Sonnet: The Token

Send me some token, that my hope may live,
  Or that my easelesse thoughts may sleep and rest;
Send me some honey to make sweet my hive,
  That in my passion I may hope the best.
I beg noe ribbond wrought with thine owne hands,
  To knit our loves in the fantastick straine
Of new-toucht youth; nor Ring to shew the stands
  Of our affection, that as that's round and plaine,
So should our loves meet in simplicity;
  No, nor the Coralls which thy wrist infold,
Lac'd up together in congruity,
  To shew our thoughts should rest in the same hold;
No, nor thy picture, though most gracious,
  And most desir'd, because best like the best;
Nor witty Lines, which are most copious,
  Within the Writings which thou hast addrest.
Send me nor this, nor that, t'increase my store,
But swear thou thinkst I love thee, and no more.

Love's Usury

For every houre that thou wilt spare mee now,
      I will allow,
Usurious God of Love, twenty to thee,
When with my browne, my gray haires equall bee;
Till then, Love, let my body raigne, and let
Mee travell, sojourne, snatch, plot, have, forget,
Resume my last yeares relict: thinke that yet
      We'had never met.

Let mee thinke any rivalls letter mine,
      And at next nine
Keepe midnights promise; mistake by the way
The maid, and tell the Lady of that delay;
Onely let mee love none, no, not the sport;
From country grasse, to comfitures of Court,
Or cities quelque choses, let report
      My minde transport.

This bargaine's good; if when I'am old, I bee
      Inflam'd by thee,
If thine owne honour, or my shame, or paine,
Thou covet most, at that age thou shalt gaine.
Doe thy will then, then subject and degree,
And fruit of love, Love I submit to thee,
Spare mee till then, I'll beare it, though she bee
      One that loves mee.

The Triple Fool

I am two fooles, I know,
  For loving, and for saying so
    In whining Poëtry;
But where's that wiseman, that would not be I,
    If she would not deny?
Then as th'earths inward narrow crooked lanes
  Do purge sea waters fretfull salt away,
I thought, if I could draw my paines,
  Through Rimes vexation, I should them allay,
Griefe brought to numbers cannot be so fierce,
For, he tames it, that fetters it in verse.

But when I have done so,
  Some man, his art and voice to show,
    Doth Set and sing my paine,
And, by delighting many, frees againe
    Griefe, which verse did restraine.
To Love, and Griefe tribute of Verse belongs,
  But not of such as pleases when'tis read,
Both are increased by such songs:
  For both their triumphs so are published,
And I, which was two fooles, do so grow three;
Who are a little wise, the best fooles bee.

Love's Infiniteness

If yet I have not all thy love,
Deare, I shall never have it all,
I cannot breath one other sigh, to move,
Nor can intreat one other teare to fall,
And all my treasure, which should purchase thee,
Sighs, teares, and oathes, and letters I have spent.
Yet no more can be due to mee,
Then at the bargaine made was ment,
If then thy gift of love were partiall,
That some to mee, some should to others fall,
    Deare, I shall never have Thee All.

Or if then thou gavest mee all,
All was but All, which thou hadst then;
But if in thy heart, since, there be or shall,
New love created bee, by other men,
Which have their stocks intire, and can in teares,
In sighs, in oathes, and letters outbid mee,
This new love may beget new feares,
For, this love was not vowed by thee.
And yet it was, thy gift being generall,
The ground, thy heart is mine, what ever shall
    Grow there, deare, I should have it all.

Yet I would not have all yet,
Hee that hath all can have no more,
And since my love doth every day admit
New growth, thou shouldst have new rewards in store;

Thou canst not every day give me thy heart,
If thou canst give it, then thou never gavest it:
Loves riddles are, that though thy heart depart,
It stayes at home, and thou with losing savest it:
But wee will have a way more liberall,
Then changing hearts, to joyne them, so wee shall
    Be one, and one anothers All.

Love's Growth

I scarce beleeve my love to be so pure
    As I had thought it was,
    Because it doth endure
Vicissitude, and season, as the grasse;
 Me thinkes I lyed all winter, when I swore,
My love was infinite, if spring make'it more.

But if this medicine, love, which cures all sorrow
With more, not onely bee no quintessence,
 But mixt of all stuffes, paining soule, or sense,
And of the Sunne his working vigour borrow,
Love's not so pure, and abstract, as they use
To say, which have no Mistresse but their Muse,
But as all else, being elemented too,
Love sometimes would contemplate, sometimes do.

And yet no greater, but more eminent,
    Love by the spring is growne;
    As, in the firmament,
Starres by the Sunne are not inlarg'd, but showne.
Gentle love deeds, as blossomes on a bough,
From loves awakened root do bud out now.

If, as in water stir'd more circles bee
Produc'd by one, love such additions take,
Those like so many spheares, but one heaven make,
For, they are all concentrique unto thee.
And though each spring doe adde to love new heate,

As princes doe in times of action get
New taxes, and remit them not in peace,
No winter shall abate the springs encrease.

The Dream

Deare love, for nothing lesse then thee
Would I have broke this happy dreame,
    It was a theame
For reason, much too strong for phantasie,
Therefore thou wakd'st me wisely; yet
My Dreame thou brok'st not, but continued'st it,
Thou art so truth, that thoughts of thee suffice,
To make dreames truths; and fables histories;
Enter these armes, for since thou thoughtst it best,
Not to dreame all my dreame, let's act the rest.

As lightning, or a Tapers light,
Thine eyes, and not thy noise wak'd mee;
    Yet I thought thee
(For thou lovest truth) an Angell, at first sight,
But when I saw thou sawest my heart,
And knew'st my thoughts, beyond an Angels art,
When thou knew'st what I dreamt, when thou knew'st
                    when
Excesse of joy would wake me, and cam'st then,
I must confesse, it could not chuse but bee
Prophane, to thinke thee any thing but thee.

Comming and staying show'd thee, thee,
But rising makes me doubt, that now,
    Thou art not thou.
That love is weake, where feare's as strong as hee;
'Tis not all spirit, pure, and brave,

If mixture it of *Feare*, *Shame*, *Honor*, have.
Perchance as torches which must ready bee,
Men light and put out, so thou deal'st with mee,
Thou cam'st to kindle, goest to come; Then I
Will dreame that hope againe, but else would die.

Love's Deity

I long to talke with some old lovers ghost,
  Who dyed before the god of Love was borne:
I cannot thinke that hee, who then lov'd most,
  Sunke so low, as to love one which did scorne.
But since this god produc'd a destinie,
And that vice-nature, custome, lets it be;
  I must love her, that loves not mee.

Sure, they which made him god, meant not so much,
  Nor he, in his young godhead practis'd it;
But when an even flame two hearts did touch,
  His office was indulgently to fit
Actives to passives. Correspondencie
Only his subject was; It cannot bee
  Love, till I love her, that loves mee.

But every moderne god will now extend
  His vast prerogative, as far as Jove.
To rage, to lust, to write to, to commend,
  All is the purlewe of the God of Love.
Oh were wee wak'ned by this Tyrannie
To ungod this child againe, it could not bee
  I should love her, who loves not mee.

Rebell and Atheist too, why murmure I,
  As though I felt the worst that love could doe?
Love might make me leave loving, or might trie
  A deeper plague, to make her love mee too,

Which, since she loves before, I'am loth to see;
Falshood is worse then hate; and that must bee,
   If shee whom I love, should love mee.

from An Anatomy of the World

She, she is dead; she's dead: when thou know'st this,
Thou know'st how poor a trifling thing man is.
And learn'st thus much by our anatomy,
The heart being perished, no part can be free.
And that except thou feed (not banquet) on
The supernatural food, religion,
Thy better growth grows withered, and scant;
Be more than man, or tho' art less an ant.

from Holy Sonnets

Annunciation

Salvation to all that will is nigh,
That all, which always is all everywhere,
Which cannot sin, and yet all sins must bear,
Which cannot die, yet cannot choose but die,
Lo, faithful virgin, yields himself to lie
In prison, in thy womb; and though he there
Can take no sin, nor thou give, yet he 'will wear
Taken from thence, flesh, which death's force may try.
Ere by the spheres time was created, thou
Wast in his mind, who is thy son, and brother,
Whom thou conceiv'st, conceived' yea thou art now
Thy maker's maker, and thy father's mother,
Tho' hast light in dark; and shutt'st in little room,
Immensity cloistered in thy dear womb.

Ascension

Salute the last and everlasting day,
Joy at the uprising of this sun, and son,
Ye whose just tears, or tribulation
Have purely washed, or burnt your drossy clay;
Behold the highest, parting hence away,
Lightens the dark clouds, which he treads upon,
Nor doth he by ascending, show alone,
But first he, and he first enters the way.
O strong ram, which hast battered heaven for me,
Mild lamb, which with thy blood, hast marked the path;
Bright torch, which shin'st, that I the way may see,
Oh, with thine own blood quench thine own just wrath,
And if thy holy Spirit, my Muse did raise,
Deign at my hands this crown of prayer and praise.

V

I am a little world made cunningly
Of Elements, and an Angelike spright,
But black sinne hath betraid to endlesse night
My worlds both parts, and (oh) both parts must die.
You which beyond that heaven which was most high
Have found new sphears, and of new lands can write,
Powre new seas in mine eyes, that so I might
Drowne my world with my weeping earnestly,
Or wash it, if it must be drown'd no more:
But oh it must be burnt! alas the fire
Of lust and envie have burnt it heretofore,
And made it fouler; Let their flames retire,
And burne me ô Lord, with a fiery zeale
Of thee and thy house, which doth in eating heale.

from Divine Meditations

1

I am a little world made cunningly
Of elements, and an angelic sprite,
But black sin hath betrayed to endless night
My world's both parts, and, oh, both parts must die.
You which beyond that heaven which was most high
Have found new spheres, and of new lands can write,
Pour news seas in mine eyes, that so I might
Drown my world with my weeping earnestly,
Or wish it if it must be drowned no more:
But oh it must be burnt; alas the fire
Of lust and envy have burnt it heretofore,
And made it fouler; let their flames retire,
And burn me O Lord, with a fiery zeal
Of thee and thy house, which doth in eating heal.

7

At the round earth's imagined corners, blow
Your trumpets, angels, and arise, arise
From death, you numberless infinities
Of souls, and to your scattered bodies go,
All whom the flood did, and fire shall o'erthrow,
All whom war, earth, age, agues, tyrannies,
Despair, law, chance, hath slain, and you whose eyes,
Shall behold God, and never taste death's woe.
But let them sleep, Lord, and me mourn a space,
For, if above all these, my sins abound,
'Tis late to ask abundance of thy grace,
When we are there' here on this lowly ground,
Teach me how to repent; for that's as good
As if thou hadst sealed my pardon, with thy blood.

Upon the Annunciation and the Passion Falling Upon One Day. 1608

Tamely, frail body' abstain today; today
My soul eats twice, Christ hither and away.
She sees him man, so like God made in this,
That of them both a circle emblem is,
Whose first and last concur; this doubtful day
Of feast or fast, Christ came, and went away;
She sees him nothing twice at once, who is all;
She sees a cedar plant itself, and fall,
Her maker put to making, and the head
Of life, at once, not yet alive, and dead;
She sees at once the virgin mother stay
Reclused at home, public at Golgotha.
Sad and rejoiced she 's seen at once, and seen
At almost fifty, and at scarce fifteen.
At once a son is promised her, and gone,
Gabriel gives Christ to her, he her to John;
Not fully a mother, she's in orbity,
At once receiver and the legacy;
All this, and all between, this day hath shown,
Th' abridgement of Christ's story, which makes one
(As in plain maps, the furthest west is east)
Of the angels' *Ave*, 'and *Consummatum est*.
How well the Church, God's court of faculties
Deals, in some times, and seldom joining these;
As by the self-fixed pole we never do
Direct our course, but the next star thereto,
Which shows where the'other is, and which we say

(Because it strays not far) doth never stray;
So God by his church, nearest to him, we know,
And stand firm, if we by her motion go;
His Spirit, as his fiery pillar doth
Lead, and his church, as cloud; to one end both:
This Church, by letting these days join, hath shown
Death and conception in mankind is one.
Or 'twas in him the same humility,
That he would be a man, and leave to be:
Or as creation he had made, as God,
With the last judgement, but one period,
His imitating spouse would join in one
Manhood's extremes: he shall come, he is gone:
Or as though one blood drop, which thence did fall,
Accepted, would have served, he yet shed all;
So though the least of his pains, deeds, or words,
Would busy a life, she all this day affords;
This treasure then, in gross, my soul unplay,
And in my life retail it every day.

from The Comparison

As the sweet sweet of roses in a still,
As that which from chafed musk cat's pores doth trill,
As the almighty balm of th' early east,
Such as the sweat drops of my mistress' breast.
And on her neck her skin such lustre sets,
They seem no sweat drops, but pearl carcanets. Rank
sweaty froth thy mistress' brow defiles,
Like spermatic issue of ripe menstruous boils,
Or like that scum, which, by need's lawless law
Enforced, Sanserra's starved men did draw
From parboiled shoes, and boots, and all the rest
Which were with any sovereign fatness blessed,
And like vile lying stones in saffroned tin,
Or warts, or weals, they hang upon her skin.
Round as the world's her head, on every side,
Like to the fatal ball which fell on Ide,
Or that whereof God had such jealousy,
As for the ravishing thereof we die.
Thy head is like a rough-hewn statue of jet,
Where marks for eyes, nose, mouth, are yet scarce set;
Like the first Chaos, or flat seeming face
Of Cynthia, when th' earth's shadows her embrace.

Illustrations

Images of John Donne.

Portrait of John Donne, c. 1595,
National Portrait Gallery, London

Portrait of John Donne at Deanery, St Paul's, 1622

Portrait of John Donne, 1630

John Donne, 1610

John Donne, St Paul's Cathedral

John Donne by Nigel Boonhma, 2012

ROBERT HERRICK

The Argument of His Book

I sing of *Brooks*, of *Blossomes, Birds*, and *Bowers*:
Of *April, May,* of *June,* and *July-Flowers.*
I sing of *May-poles, Hock-carts, Wassails, Wakes,*
Of *Bride-grooms, Brides*, and of their *Bridall-cakes.*
I write of *Youth*, of *Love*, and have Accesse
By these, to sing of cleanly-*Wantonnesse.*
I sing of *Dewes*, of *Raines*, and piece by piece
Of *Balme*, of *Oyle*, of *Spice*, and *Amber-gris.*
I sing of *Times trans-shifting*; and I write
How *Roses* first came *Red*, and *Lillies White.*
I write of *Groves*, of *Twilights*, and I sing
The Court of *Mab*, and of the *Fairie-King.*
I write of *Hell*; I sing (and ever shall)
Of *Heaven*, and hope to have it after all.

To Meddowes

Ye have been fresh and green,
    Ye have been fill'd with flower:
And ye the Walks have been
    Where Maids have spent their houres.

You have beheld, how they
    With *Wicker Arks* did come
To kisse, and beare away
    The richer Couslips home.

Y'ave heard them sweetly sing,
    And seen them in a Round:
Each Virgin, like a Spring,
    With Hony-succles crown'd.

But now, we see, none here,
    Whose silv'rie feet did tread,
And with dishevell'd Haire,
    Adorn'd this smoother mead.

Like Unthrifts, having spent,
    Your stock, and needy grown,
Y'are left here to lament
    Your poore estates, alone.

To Blossoms

Faire pledges of a fruitful Tree,
　　Why do ye fall so fast?
　　Your date is not so past;
But you may stay yet here a while,
　　To blush and gently smile;
　　　　And go at last.

What, were ye borne to be
　　An hour or half's delight;
　　And so to bid goodnight?
'Twas pitie Nature brought ye forth
　　Merely to show your worth,
　　　　And lose you quite.

But you are lovely Leaves, where we
　　May read how soon things have
　　Their end, though ne'er so brave:
And after they have shown their pride,
　　Like you a while: they Glide
　　　　Into the Grave.

To Daffodils

Faire Daffodils, we weep to see
   You haste away so soon:
As yet the early-rising Sun
   Has not attain'd his Noon.
      Stay, stay,
    Until the hasting day
       Has run
    But to the Evensong:
And having pray'd together, we
    Will go with you along

We have short time to stay, as you,
   We have as short a Spring;
As quick a growth to meet Decay,
   As you, or anything.
     We die,
    As your hours do, and dry
      Away,
    Like to the Summer's rain;
Or as the pearls of Morning's dew,
   Ne'er to be found again.

The Succession of the Four Sweet Months

First, *April*, she with mellow showers
Opens the way for early flowers;
Then after her comes smiling *May*,
In a more rich and sweet array:
Next enters *June*, and brings us more
Jems, then those two, that went before:
Then (lastly) *July* comes, and she
More wealth brings in, then all those three.

Cherry Ripe

Cherry-ripe, ripe, ripe, I cry,
Full and fair ones; come, and buy:
If so be you ask me where
They do grow? I answer, there
Where my Julia's lips do smile; –
There's the land, or cherry-isle;
Whose plantations fully show
All the year where cherries grow.

The Wake

Come *Anthea* let us two
Go to Feast, as others do.
Tarts and Custards, Creams and Cakes,
Are the Junketts still at Wakes:
Unto which the Tribes resort,
Where the business is the sport:
Morris-dancers thou shalt see,
Marian too in Pagentrie:
And a Mimick to devise
Many grinning properties.
Players there will be, and those
Base in action as in clothes:
Yet with strutting they will please
The incurious Villages.
Near the dying of the day,
There will b a *Cudgell*-Play,
Where a *Coxomb* will be broke,
Ere a good *word* can be spoke:
But the anger ends all here,
Drench't in Ale, or drown'd in Beer.
Happy Rusticks, best content
With the cheapest Meriment:
And possess no other feare,
Then to want the Wake next Year.

The Lily in a Christal

You have beheld a smiling *Rose*
    When Virgins hands have drawn
    O'r it a Cobweb-Lawne:
And here, you see, this Lily shows,
    Tomb'd in a *Christal* stone,
More fair in this transparent case,
    Then when it grew alone;
    And had but single grace.

You see how *Cream* but naked is;
    Nor dances in the eye
    Without a Strawberrie:
Or some fine tincture, like to this,
    Which draws the sight thereto,
More by that wantoning with it;
    Then when the paler hue
    No mixture did admit.

You see how *Amber* through the streams
    More gently strokes the sight,
    With some conceal'd delight;
Then when he darts his radiant beams
    Into the boundless air:
Where either too much light his worth
    Doth all at once impair,
    Or set it little forth.
Put Purple Grapes, or Cherries in-

To Glasse, and they will send
            More beauty to commend
Them, from that cleane and subtile skin,
            Then if they naked stood,
And had no other pride at all,
            But their own flesh and blood,
            And tinctures natural.

Thus Lily, Rose, Grape, Cherry, Cream,
            And Strawberrie do stir
            More love, when they transfer
A weak, a soft, a broken beam:
            Then if they sho'd discover
At full their proper excellence;
            Without some Scene cast over,
            To juggle with the sense.

Thus let this *Christal'd Lily* be
            A Rule, how far to teach,
            Your nakedness must reach:
And that, no further, then we see
            Those glaring colours laid
By Arts wise hand, but to this end
            They sho'd obey a shade;
            Lest they too far extend.

So though y'are white as Swan, or Snow,
            And have the power to move
            A world of men to love:
Yet, when your Lawns & Silks shall flow;
            And that white cloud divide
Into a doubtful Twilight; then,

Then will your hidden Pride
Raise greater fires in men.

To *Phillis* to Love, and Live With Him

Live, live with me, and thou shalt see
The pleasures I'll prepare for thee:
What sweets the Country can afford
Shall blesse thy Bed, and blesse thy Board.
The soft sweet Mosse shall be thy bed,
With crawling Woodbine over-spread:
By which the silver-shedding streames
Shall gently melt thee into dreames.
Thy clothing next, shall be a Gowne
Made of the Fleeces purest Downe.
The tongues of Kids shall be thy meate;
Their Milke thy drinke; and thou shalt eate
The Pastes of Filberts for thy bread
With Cream of Cowslips buttered:
Thy Feasting-Tables shall be Hills
With *Daisies* spread, and *Daffadils*;
Where thou shalt sit, and *Red-brest* by,
For meat, shall give thee melody.
I'll give thee Chaines and Carkanets
Of *Primroses* and *Violets*.
A Bag and Bottle thou shalt have;
That richly wrought, and This as brave;
So that as either shall expresse
The Wearer's no meane Shepheardesse.
At Sheering-times, and yearely Wakes,
When *Themilis* his pastime makes,
There thou shalt be; and be the wit,
Nay more, the Feast, and grace of it.

On holy-dayes, when Virgins meet
To dance the Heyes with nimble feet;
Thou shalt come forth, and then appeare
Then *Queen of Roses* for that yeere.
And having danc't ('bove all the best)
Carry the Garland from the rest.
In Wicker-baskets Maids shall bring
To thee, (my dearest Shepharling)
The blushing Apple, bashfull Peare,
And shame-fac't Plum, (all simp'ring there).
Walk in the Groves, and thou shalt find
The name of *Phillis* in the Rind
Of every straight, and smooth-skin tree;
Where kissing that, I'll twice kisse thee.
To thee a Sheep-hook I will send,
Be-pranckt with Ribbands, to this end,
This, this alluring Hook might be
Lesse for to catch a sheep, then me.
Thou shalt have Possets, Wassails fine,
Not made of Ale, but spiced Wine;
To make thy Maids and selfe free mirth,
All sitting neer the glitt'ring hearth.
Thou sha't have Ribbands, Roses, Rings,
Gloves, Garters, Stockings, Shooes, and Strings
Of winning Colours, that shall move
Others to Lust, but me to Love.
These (nay) and more, thine own shall be,
If thou wilt love, and live with me.

The Vision to *Electra*

I dream'd we both were in a bed
Of Roses, almost smothered:
The warmth and sweetness had me there
Made lovingly familiar,
But that heard thy sweet breath say
Faults done by night will blush by day.
I kissed thee (panting), and I call
Night to the Record! that was all.
But, ah! if empty dreams so please,
Love give me more such nights as these.

Mrs *Elizabeth Wheeler*, Under the Name of the Lost Sephardesse

Among the *Myrtles*, as I walkt,
Love and my sighs thus intertalkt:
Tell me, said I, in deep distresse,
Where I may find my Shepardesse.
Thou foole, said Love, know'st thou not this?
In every thing that's sweet, she is.
In yond' *Carnation* go and seek,
There thou shalt find her lip and cheek:
In that ennamel'd *Pansie* by,
There thou shalt have her curious eye:
In bloome of *Peach*, and *Roses* bud,
There waves the Streamer of her blood.
'Tis true, said I, and thereupon
I went to pluck them one by one,
To make of parts an union;
But on a sudden all were gone.
At which I stopt; Said Love, these be
The true resemblances of thee;
For as these flowers, thy joyes must die,
And in the turning of an eye;
And all thy hopes of her must wither,
Like those short sweets ere knit together.

from The Apparition of His Mistress Calling Him to Elysium

Come then, and like two Doves with silv'ry wings,
Let our souls fly to th' shades where ever springs
Sit smiling in the Meads; where Balm and Oil,
Roses and cassia crown the untill'd soil.
Where no disease reigns, or infection comes
To blast the Air, but *Ambergris* and *Gums*.
This, that, and ev'ry Thicket doth transpire
More sweet than *Storax* from the hallowed fire;
Where ev'ry tree a wealthy issue bears
Of fragrant Apples, blushing Plums, or Peares;
And all the shrubs, with sparkling spangles, show
Like Morning Sunshine tinselling the dew.
Here in green Meddowes sits eternal May,
Purfling the Margents, while perpetual Day
So double gilds the Air, as that no night
Can ever rust th'Enamel of the light.
Here, naked Younglings, handsome Striplings, run
Their Goales for Virgins' kisses; which when done,
Then unto Dancing forth the learned Round
Commix'd they meet, with endless Roses crown'd.
And here we'll sit on Primrose-banks, and see
Love's *Chorus* led by *Cupid*; and we'll be
Two loving followers, too, unto the Grove
Where Poets sing the stories of our love.

His Mistress To Him At His Farewell

You may vow I'll not forget
To pay the debt
Which to thy memory stands as due
As faith can seal it you.
 – Take then tribute of my tears;
So long as I have fears
To prompt me, I shall ever
Languish and look, but thy return see never.
Oh then to lessen my despair,
Print thy lips into(the air,
So by this
Means, I may kiss thy kiss,
Whenas some kind
Wind
Shall hither waft it: – And, in lieu,
My lips shall send a thousand back to you.

To the most fair and lovely Mistress, *Anne Soame*, now *Lady Abdie*

So smell those odours that do rise
From out the wealthy spiceries:
So smells the flower of *blooming Clove*;
Or *Roses* smother'd in the stove:
So smells the Aire of spiced wine;
Or *Essences* of *Jessimine*:
So smells the Breath about the hives,
When well the work of honey thrives;
And all the *busie Factours* come
Laden with wax and honey home:
So smell those neat and woven Bowers,
All over-archt with *Orange flowers*,
And *Almond blossoms*, that do mix
To make rich these *Aromatikes*:
So smell those bracelets, and those bands
Of *Amber* chaf't between the hands,
When thus enkindled they transpire
A noble perfume from the fire.
The wine of cherries, and to these,
The cooling breath of Respasses;
The smell of mornings milk, and cream;
Butter of *Cowslips* mixt with them;
Of roasted warden, or bak'd pear,
These are not to be reckon'd here;
When as the meanest part of her,
Smells like the maiden-Pomander.

Thus sweet she smells, or what can be
More lik'd by her, or lov'd by me.

Love Lightly Pleased

Let fair or foul my mistress be,
Or low, or tall, she pleaseth me;
Or let her walk, or stand, or sit,
The posture her's, I'm pleased with it;
Or let her tongue be still, or stir
Graceful is every thing from her;
Or let her grant, or else deny,
My love will fit each history.

Of Love: A Sonnet

How Love came in, I do not know,
Whether by th'eye, or ear, or no;
Or whether with the soul it came,
At first, infused with the same;
Whether in part 'tis here or there,
Or, like the soul, whole every where.
This troubles me; but I as well
As any other, this can tell;
That when from hence she does depart,
The outlet then is from the heart.

His Protestation to *Perilla*

Noonday and Midnight shall at once be seen:
Trees, at one time, shall be both sere and green:
Fire and water shall together lie
In one self-sweet-conspiring sympathy:
Summer and Winter shall at one time show
Ripe ears of corn, and up to th' ears in snow:
Seas shall be sandless; fields devoid of grass;
Shapeless the world, (as when all *Chaos* was)
Before my dear *Perilla*, I will be
False to my vow, or fall away from thee.

To *Anthea*

Come *Anthea*, know thou this,
Love at no time idle is:
Let's be doing, though we play
But at push-pin (half the day:)
Chains of sweetbents let us make,
Captive one, or both, to take:
In which bondage we will lie,
Soules transfusing thus, and die.

Art Above Nature; To *Julia*

When I behold a Forest spread
With silken trees upon thy head,
And when I see that other Dress
Of flowers set in comeliness:
When I behold another grace
In the ascent of curious Lace,
Which like a Pinnacle doth show
The top, and the top-gallant too.
Then, when I see thy Tresses bound
Into an Oval, square, or round;
And knit in knots far more than I
Can tell by tongue, or true-love tie:
Next, when those Lawny Films I see
Play with a wild civility:
And all those airy silks to flow,
Alluring me, and tempting so:
I must confess, mine eye and heart
Dotes less on Nature, than on Art.

To *Julia*

Permit me, *Julia*, now to go away;
Or by thy love, decree me here to stay.
If thou wilt say, that I shall live with thee;
Here shall my endless Tabernacle be:
If not, (as beautiful) I will live alone
There, where no language ever yet was known.

To *Julia*

How rich and pleasing thou my *Julia* art
In each thy dainty, and peculiar part!
First, thy *Queen-ship* on thy head is set
Of flowers a sweet commingled Coronet:
About thy neck a Carkanet is bound,
Made of the *Rubie, Pearle* and *Diamond*:
A golden ring, that shines upon thy thumb:
About thy wrist, the rich *Dardanium*.
Between thy Breasts (than Down of Swans more
                                        white)
There plays the *Sapphire* with the *Chrysolite*.
No part besides must of thy selfe be known,
But by the *Topaz, Opal, Calcedon.*

Upon *Julia's* Unlacing Herself

Tell, if thou canst, (and truly) whence doth come
This *Camphire, Storax, Spiknard, Galbanum*:
These *Musks*, these *Ambers*, and those other smells
(Sweet as the *vestrie of the Oracles*.)
I'll tell thee; while my *Julia* did unlace
Her silken bodies, but a breathing space:
The passive Aire such odour then assum'd,
As when to *Jove* Great *Juno* goes perfum'd.
Whose pure-Immortal body doth transmit
A scent, that fills both Heaven and Earth with it.

The Night-Piece to *Julia*

Her Eyes the Glow-worm lend thee,
The Shooting Starres attend thee;
      And the Elves also,
      Whose little eyes glow
Like the sparks of fire, befriend thee.

No *Will-o'-the-Wispe* mislight thee,
Nor Snake or Slow-worm bite thee;
      But on, on thy way
      Not making a stay,
Since Ghost there's none to affright thee.

Let not the dark thee cumber:
What though the Moon does slumber?
      The Starres of the night
      Will lend thee their light
Like Tapers clear without number.

Then *Julia*, let me woo thee,
Thus, thus to come unto me;
      And when I shall meet
      Thy silv'ry feet
My soul I'll pour into thee.

The *Maiden-blush*

So look the mornings when the Sun
Paints them with fresh Vermilion:
So Cherries blush, and Kathern Peares,
And Apricocks, in youthful yeares:
So Corralls looke more lovely Red,
And Rubies lately polished:
So purest Diaper doth shine,
Stain'd by the Beames of Claret wine:
As *Julia* looks when she doth dress
Her either cheeke with bashfulness.

Julia's *Petticoat*

Thy Azure Robe I did behold,
As airy as the leaves of gold,
Which, erring here, and wand'ring there,
Pleas'd with transgression everywhere:
Sometimes 'twould pant, and sigh, and heave,
As if to stir it scarce had leave:
But having got it; thereupon
'Twould make a brave expansion.
And pound'd with stars it show'd to me
Like a *Celestiall Canopie*.
Sometimes 'twould blaze, and then abate,
Like to a flame grown moderate:
Sometimes away 'twould wildly fling,
Then to thy thighs so closely cling
That some conceit did melt me down,
As lovers fall into a swoon:
And, all confus'd, I there did lie
Drown'd in Delights, but could not die.
That Leading Cloud I follow'd still,
Hoping t'have seen of it my fill;
But ah! I could not: should it move
To Life Eternal, I could love.

Upon *Julia's* Clothes

When as in silks my *Julia* goes,
Then, then (me thinks) how sweetly flowes
That liquefaction of her clothes.

Next, when I cast mine eyes and see
That brave Vibration each way free;
O how that glittering taketh me!

To *Julia*, in Her Dawn, or Daybreak

By the next kindling of the day
   My *Julia* thou shalt see,
Ere *Ave-Mary* thou canst say
   I'll come and visit thee.

Yet ere thou counsl'st with thy Glasse,
   Appeare thou to mine eyes
As smooth, and nak't, as she that was
   The prime of *Paradise*.

If blush thou must, then blush thou through
   A Lawn, that thou mayst looke
As purest Pearles, or Pebbles do
   When peeping through a Brooke.

As Lilies shrin'd in Christall, so
   Do thou to me appeare;
Or Damask Roses, when they grow
   To sweet acquaintance there.

Delight in Disorder

A sweet disorder in the dress
Kindles in clothes a wantonness:
A Lawn about the shoulders thrown
Into a fine distraction:
An erring Lace which here and there
Enthralls the Crimson Stomacher:
A Cuff neglectful, and thereby
Ribands to flow confusedly:
A winning wave (deserving Note)
In the tempestuous petticoat:
A careless shoestring, in whose tie
I see a wild civility:
Do more bewitch me, than when Art
Is too precise in every part.

A Meditation For His Mistress

You are a *Tulip* seen today,
But (Dearest) of so short a stay
That where you grew scarce man can say.

You are a lovely *July-flower*
Yet one rude wind or ruffling shower
Will force you hence, (and in an hour.)

You are a sparkling *Rose* in' th'bud,
Yet lost ere that chaste flesh and blood
Can show where you or grew or stood.

You are a full-spread, fair-set Vine,
And can with Tendrils love entwine,
Yet dry'd, ere you distil your Wine.

You are like Balme enclosed (well)
In *Amber*, or some *Crystal* shell,
Yet lost ere you transfuse your smell.

You are a dainty *Violet*,
Yet whither'd ere you can be set
Within a Virgin's Coronet.

You are the *Queen* all flowers among,
But die you must (fair Maid) ere long,
As He, the maker of this song.

To His Mistress (Objecting to Him Neither Toying or Talking)

You say I love not, 'cause I do not play
Still with your curls, and kiss the time away.
You blame me too, because I can't devise
Some sport, to please those Babies in your eyes:
By *Love's Religion*, I must here confess it,
The most I love, when I the least express it.
Small griefs find tongues: Full Casks are ever found
To give (if any, yet) but little sound.
Deep waters noiseless are; and this we know,
That chiding streams betray small depth below.
So when Love speechless is, she doth expresse
A depth in love, and that depth, bottomlesse.
Now since my love is tongueless, know me such,
Who speak but little, 'cause I love so much.

A Conjuration, to *Electra*

By those soft Tods of wool
With which the air is full:
By all those Tinctures there,
That paint the *Hemisphere*:
By Dews and drizzling Rain,
That swell the Golden Grain:
By all those sweets that he
I' the flow'ry Nunnery:
By silent Nights, and the
Three Forms of Hecate:
By all Aspects that bless
The sober *Sorceress*,
While juice she strains, and pith
To make her Philtres with:
By Time, that hastens on
Things to perfection:
And by your self, the best
Conjurement of the rest:
Of my *Electra*! be
In love with none, but me.

To *Electra*

I dare not ask a kisse;
   I dare not beg a smile;
Lest having that, or this,
   I might grow proud the while.

No, no, the utmost share
   Of my desire, shall be
Only to kisse that Aire,
   That lately kissed thee.

Lovers, How They Come and Part

A *Gyges'* Ring they bear about them still,
To be, and not seen when and where they will.
They tread on clouds, and though they sometimes fall,
They fall like dew, but make no noise at all.
So silently they one to th'other come,
As colours steal into the Pear or Plum,
And Air-like, leave no pression to be seen
Where e'er they met, or parting place has been.

To Sylvia, To Wed

Let us, though late, at last, my Silvia, wed;
And loving lie in one devoted bed.
Thy watch may stand, my minutes fly post haste;
No sound calls back the year that once is past.
Then, sweetest Silvia, let's no longer stay;
True love, we know, precipitates delay.
Away with doubts, all scruples hence remove!
No man, at one time, can be wise, and love.

On a Perfumed Lady

You say you're sweet: how should we know
Whether that you be sweet or no?
 – From powders and perfumes keep free;
Then we shall smell how sweet you be!

To the Maids to Walk Abroad

Come sit we under yonder Tree,
Where merry as the Maids we'll be.
And as on *Primroses* we sit,
We'll venter (if we can) at wit:
If not, at *Draw-gloves* we will play;
So spend some minutes of the day:
Or else spin out the thread of sands,
Playing at *Questions* and *Commands*:
Or tell what strange Tricks Love can do,
By quickly making one of two.
Thus we will sit and talk; but tell
No cruel truths of *Philomell*,
Of *Phillis*, whom hard Fate forc't on,
To kill her selfe for *Demophon*.
But Fables we'll relate; how *Jove*
Put on all shapes to get a Love:
As now a *Satyr*, then a *Swan*;
A *Bull* but then; and now a man.
Next we will act, how young men woe;
And sigh, and kiss, as Lovers do:
And talk of Brides; & who shall make
That wedding-smock, this bridal-Cake;
That Dress, this Sprig, that Leaf, this Vine;
That smooth and silken Columbine.
This done, we'll draw lots, who shall buy
And guild the Baies and Rosemary:
What Posies for our Wedding Rings;
What Gloves we'll give, and Ribanings:

And smiling at ourselves, decree,
Who then the joining *Priest* shall be.
What short sweet Prayers shall be said;
And how the Possets all be made
With Cream of Lilies (not of Kine)
And *Maiden's-blush*, for spiced wine.
Thus, having talkt, we'll next commend
A kiss to each; and *so we'll end*.

Corinna's Going a-Maying

Get up, get up for shame, the Blooming Morn
Upon her wings presents the god unshorn.
  See how *Aurora* throws her fair
  Fresh-quilted colours through the air:
  Get up, sweet-Slug-a-bed, and see
  The Dew bespangled Herb and Tree.
Each flower has wept and bow'd towards the East
Above an hour since: yet you not dress'd;
  Nay! not so much as out of bed?
  When all the birds have Matins said
  And sung their thankful Hymns, 'tis sin,
  Nay, profanation to keep in,
When as a thousand Virgins on this day
Spring, sooner than the Lark, to fetch in May.

Rise and put on your Foliage, and be seen
To come forth, like the Spring-time, fresh and green,
  And sweet as *Flora*. Take no care
  For jewels for your Gown or Hair:
  Fear not; the leaves will strew
  Gems in abundance upon you:
Besides, the childhood of the Day has kept,
Against you come, some *Orient Pearls* unwept;
  Come and receive them while the light
  Hangs on the Dew-locks of the night:
  And *Titan* on the Eastern hill
  Retires himself, or else stands still
Till you come forth. Wash, dress, be brief in praying:

Few Beads are best when once we go a-Maying.

Come, my *Corinna*, come; and, coming, mark
How each field turns a street, each street a Park
   Made green and trimm'd with trees: see
       how
   Devotion gives each House a Bough
   Or Branch: Each Porch, each door ere this
   An Ark, a Tabernacle is,
Made up of white-thorn neatly interwove;
As if here were those cooler shades of love.
   Can such delights be in the street
   And open fields and we not see't?
   Come, we'll abroad; and let's obey
   The Proclamation made for May:
And sin no more, as we have done, by staying;
But, my *Corinna*, come, let's go a-Maying.

There's not a budding Boy or Girl this day
But is got up, and gone to bring in May.
   A deal of youth, ere this, is come
   Back, and with *White-thorn* laden home.
   Some have despatch'd their Cakes and
       Cream
   Before that we have left to dream:
And some have wept, and woo'd, and plighted Troth,
And chose their Priest, ere we can cast off sloth:
   Many a green-gown has been given;
   Many a kiss, both odd and even:
   Many a glance too has been sent
   From out the eye, Love's Firmament;
Many a jest told of the Keys betraying

This night, and Locks pick'd, yet we're not a-Maying.

Come, let us go while we are in our prime;
And take the harmless folly of the time,
> We shall grow old apace, and die
> Before we know our liberty.
> Our life I short, and our days run
> As fast away as does the sun;
And, as a vapour or a drop of rain,
Once lost, can ne'er be found again,
> So when or you or I are made
> A fable, song, or fleeting shade,
> All love, all liking, all delight
> Lies drowned with us in endless night.
Then while time serves, and we are but decaying,
Come, my *Corinna*, come, let's go a-Maying.

Another Grace For A Child

Here a little child I stand
Heaving up my either hand;
Cold as paddocks though they be,
Here I lift them up to Thee,
For a benison to fall
On our meat, and on us all. Amen.

To Music. A Song

Music, thou *Queen of Heaven*, Care-charming-spell,
    That strik'st a stilnesse into hell:
Thou that tam'st *Tygers*, and fierce storms (that rise)
    With thy soul-melting Lullabies:
Fall down, down, down, from those thy chiming
                      spheres,
To charme our soules, as thou enchant'st our eares.

To the Virgins, to Make Much of Time

Gather ye Rose-buds while ye may,
　　Old Time is still a flying:
And this same flower that smiles today,
　　Tomorrow will be dying.

The glorious Lamp of Heaven, the Sun,
　　The high he's a getting;
The sooner will his Race be run,
　　And nearer he's to Setting.

That Age is best, which is the first,
　　When Youth and Blood are warmer;
But being spent, the worse, and worst
　　Times, still succeed the former.

Then be not coy, but use your time;
　　And while ye may, goe marry:
For having lost but once your prime,
　　You may forever tarry.

The Eye

Make me a heaven; and make me there
Many a less and greater spheare.
Make me the straight, and oblique lines;
The Motions, Lations, and the Signes.
Make me a Chariot, and a Sun;
And let them through a Zodiac run:
Next, place me Zones, and Tropicks there;
With all the Seasons of the Yeare.
Make me a Sun-set; and a Night:
And then present the Mornings-light
Cloath'd in her Chamlets of Delight.
To these, make Clouds to poure downe raine;
With weather foule, then faire againe.
And when, wise Artist, that thou hast,
With all that can be, this heaven grac't;
Ah! what is then this curious skie,
But only my *Corinna's* eye?

His Return to London

From the dull confines of the drooping West,
To see the day spring from the pregnant East,
Ravisht in spirit, I come, nay more, I flie
To thee, blest place of my Nativitie!
Thus, thus with hallowed foot I touch the ground,
With thousand blessings by thy Fortune crown'd.
O fruitful Genius! that bestowest here
An everlasting plenty, yeere by yeere.
O *Place!* O *People!* Manners! fram'd to please
All *Nations, Customes, Kindreds, Languages!*
I am a free-born *Roman*; suffer then,
That I amongst you live a Citizen.
London my home is: though by hard fate sent
Into a long and irksome banishment;
Yet since call'd back; henceforward let me be,
O native country, repossest by thee!
For, rather then I'll to the West return,
I'll beg of thee first here to have mine Urn.
Weak I am grown, and must in short time fall;
Give thou my sacred Reliques Burial.

His Tears to *Thamasis*

I send, I send here my supremest kiss
To thee my *silver-footed Thamasis*.
No more shall I reiterate thy Strand,
Whereon so many Stately Structures stand:
Nor in the summers sweeter evenings go,
To bath in thee (as thousand others doe.)
No more shall I along thy christall glide,
In Barge (with boughs and rushes beautifi'd)
With soft-smooth Virgins (for our chast disport)
To *Richmond, Kingstone*, and to *Hampton-Court*:
Never again shall I with Finnie-Ore
Put from, or draw unto the faithful shore:
And Landing here, or safely Landing there,
Make way to my *Beloved Westminster*:
Or to the *Golden-cheap-side*, where the earth
Of *Julia Herrick* gave to me my Birth.
May all clean *Nymphs* and curious water Dames,
With Swan-like-state, float up & down thy streams:
No drought upon thy wanton waters fall
To make them Leane, and languishing at all.
No ruffling winds come hither to disease
Thy pure, and *Silver-wristed Naides*.
Keep up your state ye streams; and as ye spring,
Never make sick your Banks by surfeiting.
Grow young with Tides, and though I see ye never,
Receive this vow, *so fare-ye-well for ever.*

Poets

Wantons we are; and though our words be such,
Our Lives do differ from our Lines by much.

On Love

Love's of itself too sweet; the best of all
Is, when love's honey has a dash of gall.

Silence

Suffer thy legs, but not thy tongue to walk:
God, the most Wise, is sparing of His talk.

Presence and Absence

When what is lov'd, is Present, love doth spring;
But being absent, Love lies languishing.

Another Upon Her Weeping

She by the River sat, and sitting there,
She wept, and made it deeper by a teare.

Dreams

Here we are all, by day; By night, w'are hurl'd
By dreams, each one, into a sev'rall world.

Life Is the Body's Light

Life is the body's light; which, once declining,
Those crimson clouds i' th' cheeks and lips leave
                        shining:-
Those counter-changed tabbies in the air,
The sun once set, all of one colour are:
So, when death comes, fresh tinctures lose their
                        place,
And dismal darkness then doth smutch the face.

Discontents In Devon

More discontents I never had
Since I was born, than here;
Where I have been, and still am, sad,
In this dull Devonshire.
Yet justly too I must confess,
I ne'er invented such
Ennobled numbers for the press,
Than where I loath'd so much.

The Departure of the Good *Dæmon*

What can I do in Poetry,
Now the good Spirit's gone from me?
Why nothing now, but lonely sit,
And over-read what I have writ.

His Poetrie His Pillar

Only a little more
    I have to write,
    Then I'll give o're,
And bid the world Goodnight.

'Tis but a flying minute,
    That I must stay,
    Or linger in it;
And then I must away.

O time that cut'st down all!
    And scarce leav'st here
    Memorial
Of any men that were.

How many lye forgot
    In Vaults beneath?
    And piecemeal rot
Without a fame in death?

Behold this living stone,
    I fear for me,
    Ne'r to be thrown
Downe, envious Time by thee.

Pillars let some set up,
    (If so they please)

Here is my hope,
And my *Pyramids*.

To Find God

Weigh me the fire; or canst thou find
A way to measure out the Wind;
Distinguish all those Floods that are
Mix'd in that watrie theatre;
And taste thou them as saltlesse there
As in their channel first they were.
Tell me the People that do keep
Within the Kingdoms of the Deep;
Or fetch me back that Cloud again
Beshiver'd into seeds of Rain;
Tell me the motes, dust, sands, and spears
Of corn, when Summer shakes his ears;
Show me that world of Starres, and whence
They noiseless spill their Influence:
This if thou canst, then show me Him
That rides the glorious *Cherubim*.

On Heaven

Permit mine eyes to see
Part, or the whole of Thee,
   O happy place!
   Where all have Grace,
   And Garlands shar'd,
   For their reward;
   Where each chaste Soul
   In long, white stole,
   And Palmes in hand,
   Do ravisht stand;
   So in a ring,
   The praises sing
   Of Three in One,
   That fill the Throne;
While Harps, and Viols then
To Voices, say, *Amen*.

Eternitie

O years! and Age! Farewell:
　　Behold I go,
　　Where I do know
Infinitie to dwell.

And these mine eyes shall see
　　All times, how they
　　Are lost i'th'Sea
Of vast Eternitie.

Where never Moone shall sway
　　The Starres; but she,
　　And Night, shall be
Drown'd in one endlesse Day.

Upon Parting

Go hence away, and in thy parting know
Tis not my voice, but heavens, that bids thee go;
Spring hence thy faith, nor thinke it ill desert
I find in thee, that makes me thus to part,
But voice of fame, and voice of heaven have
thunder'd
We both were, if both of us not sunder'd;
Fold now thine arms, and in thy last look reare
One Sigh of love, and coole it with a teare;
Since part we must Let's kisse, that done retire
With as cold frost, as erst we met with fire;
With such white vows as fate can ne'er dissever
But truth knit fast; and so farewell for ever.

To His Booke

Go thou forth my booke, though late;
Yet be timely fortunate.
It may chance good-luck may send
Thee a kinsman, or a friend,
That may harbour thee, when I,
With my fates neglected lye.
If thou know'st not where to dwell,
See, the fire's by: *Farewell*.

Illustrations

Images of Robert Herrick and art based on his work.

Title pages of Hesperides by Robert Herrick
(this page and over)

HESPERIDES:
OR,
THE WORKS
BOTH
HUMANE & DIVINE
OF
ROBERT HERRICK *Esq.*

OVID.

Effugient avidos Carmina nostra Rogos.

LONDON,
Printed for *John Williams,* and *Francis Eglesfield.*
and are to be fold by *Tho: Hunt,* Book-feller
in *Exon.* 1648.

John William Waterhouse, Gather Ye Rosebuds While Ye May,
1909, private collection

John William Waterhouse, Gather Ye Rosebuds While Ye May, 1909

John William Waterhouse, Ophelia (Gather Ye Rosebuds
While Ye May), 1909

Elizabeth Stanhope Forbes, A Sweet Disorder In the Dress, 1897-98

HENRY VAUGHAN

The World

1

I saw Eternity the other night
Like a great *Ring* of pure and endless light,
    All calm, as it was bright,
And round beneath it, Time in hours, days, years
    Driven by the spheres
Like a vast shadow moved, in which the world
    And all her train were hurled;
The doting lover in his quaintest strain
    Did there complain,
Near him, his lute, his fancy, and his flights,
    Wit's sour delights,
With gloves, and knots the silly snares of pleasure
    Yet his dear treasure
All scattered lay, while he his eyes did pour
    Upon a flower.

2

The darksome states-man hung with weights and woe
Like a thick midnight-fog moved there so slow
    He did nor stay, nor go;
Condemning thoughts (like sad eclipses) scowl
    Upon his soul,
And clouds of crying witnesses without
    Pursued him with one shout.
Yet digged the mole, and lest his ways be found

Worked under ground,
Where he did clutch his prey, but one did see
    That policy,
Churches and altars fed him, perjuries
    Were gnats and flies,
It rained about him blood and tears, but he
    Drank them as free.

3

The fearful miser on a heap of rust
Sat pining all his life there, did scarce trust
    His own hands with the dust,
Yet would not place one piece above, but lives
    In fear of thieves.
Thousands there were as frantic as himself
    And hugged each one his pelf,
The down-right epicure placed heaven in sense
    And scorned pretence
While others slipped into a wide excess
    Said little less;
The weaker sort slight, trivial wares enslave
    Who think them brave,
And poor, despised truth sat counting by
    Their victory.

4

Yet some, who all this while did weep and sing,
And sing, and weep, soared up into the *Ring*,
    But most would use no wing.
O fools (said I,) thus to prefer dark night
    Before true light,
To live in grots, and caves, and hate the day
    Because it shows the way,
The way which from this dead and dark abode
    Leads up to God,
A way where you might tread the sun, and he
    More bright than he.
But as I did their madness so discuss
    One whispered thus,
This ring the bride-groom did for none provide
    But for his bride.

'They are all gone into the world of light!'

They are all gone into the world of light!
   And I alone sit ling'ring here;
Their very memory is fair and bright,
    And my sad thoughts doth clear.

It glows and glitters in my cloudy breast
   Like stars upon some gloomy grove,
Or those faint beams in which this hill is dressed,
   After the sun's remove.

I see them walking in an air of glory,
   Whose light doth trample on my days:
My days, which are at best but dull and hoary,
    Mere glimmering and decays.

O holy hope! and high humility,
   High as the heavens above!
These are your walks, and you have showed them me
    To kindle my cold love,

Dear, beauteous death! the jewel of the just,
   Shining nowhere, but in the dark;
What mysteries do lie beyond thy dust;
    Could man outlook that mark!

He that hath found some fledged bird's nest, may know
   At first sight, if the bird be flown;

But what fair well, or grove he sings in now,
  That is to him unknown.

And yet, as Angels in some brighter dreams
  Call to the soul, when man doth sleep:
So some strange thoughts transcend our wonted
                                    themes,
    And into glory peep.

If a star were confined into a tomb
  Her captive flames must needs burn there;
But when the hand that locked her up, gives room
    She'll shine through all the sphere.

Of Father of eternal life, and all
  Created glories under thee!
Resume thy spirit from this world of thrall
    Into true liberty.

Either disperse these mists, which blot and fill
  My perspective (still) as they pass,
Or else remove me hence unto that hill,
    Where I shall need no glass.

The Night

Through that pure *Virgin-shrine,*
That sacred veil drawn o'er thy glorious noon
That men might look and live as glow-worms shine,
    And face the moon:
  Wise *Nicodemus* saw such light
  As made him know his God by night.

    Most blest believer he!
Who in that land of darkness and blind eyes
Thy long expected healing wings could see,
    When thou didst rise,
  And what can nevermore be done,
  Did at mid-night speak with the Sun!

    O who will tell me, where
He found thee at that dead and silent hour!
What hallowed solitary ground did bear
    So rare a flower,
  Within whose sacred leaves did lie
  The fullness of the Deity.

    No mercy-seat of gold,
No dead and dusty *Cherub*, nor carved stone,
But his own living works did my Lord hold
    And lodge alone;
  Where *trees* and *herbs* did watch and peep
  And wounds, while the *Jews* did sleep.

Dear night! this world's defeat;
The stop to busy fools; care's check and curb;
The day of Spirits; my soul's calm retreat
    Which none disturb!
  Christ's progress, and his prayer time;
  The hours to which high Heaven doth chime.

    God's silent, searching flight:
When my Lord's head is filled with dew, and all
His locks are wet with the clear drops of night;
    His still, soft call;
  His knocking time; the soul's dumb watch,
  When Spirits their fair kindred catch.

    Were all my loud, evil days
Calm and unhaunted as is thy dark Tent,
Whose peace but by some *Angel's* wing or voice
    Is seldom rent;
  Then I in Heaven all the long year
  Would keep, and never wander here.

    But living where the sun
Doth all things wake, and where all mix and tire
Themselves and others,I consent and run
    To every mire,
  And by this world's ill-guiding light,
  Err more than I can do by night.

    There is in God (some say)
A deep, but dazzling darkness; as men here
Say it is late and dusky, because they
    See not all clear;

* *167*

O for that night! where I in him
Might live invisible and dim.

The Morning-Watch

O joys! infinite sweetness! with what flowers,
And shoots of glory, my soul breaks, and buds!
      All the long hours
      Of night, and rest
      Through the still shrouds
      Of sleep, and clouds,
    This dew fell on my breast;
      Of how it *blows*,
And *spirits* all my earth! hark! In what rings,
And *hymning circulations* the quick world
      Awakes, and sings;
      The rising winds,
      And falling springs,
      Birds, beasts, all things
    Adore him in their kinds.
      Thus all is hurled
In sacred *hymns*, and *order*, the great *chime*
And *symphony* of nature. Prayer is
      The world in tune,
      A spirit-voice,
      And vocal joys
    Whose *echo is* heaven's bliss.
      O let me climb
When I lie down! The pious soul by night
Is like a clouded star, whose beams though said
      To shed their light
      Under some cloud
      Yet are above,

And shine, and move
Beyond that misty shroud.
So in my bed
That curtained grave, though sleep, like ashes, hide
My lamp, and life, both shall in thee abide.

The Retreat

Happy those early days! when I
Shined in my Angel-infancy.
Before I understood this place
Appointed for my second race,
Or taught my soul to fancy aught
But a white, celestial thought,
When yet I had not walked above
A mile, or two, from my first love,
And looking back (at that short space,)
Could see a glimpse of his bright-face;
When on some *gilded cloud*, or *flower*
My gazing souls would dwell an hour,
And in those weaker glories spy
Some shadows of eternity;
Before I taught my tongue to wound
My conscience with a sinful sound,
Or had the black art to dispense
A several sin to every sense,
But felt through all this fleshly dress
Bright *shoots* of everlastingness.
    O how I long to travel back
And tread against that ancient track!
That I might once more reach that plain,
Where first I left my glorious train,
From whence the enlightened spirits sees
That shady city of palm trees;
But (ah!) my soul with too much stay
Is drunk, and staggers in the way.

Some men a forward motion love,
But I by backward steps would move,
And when this dust falls to the urn
In that state I came return.

To the River Isca

When *Daphne's* lover here first wore the *bays*,
Eurotas' secret streams heard all his *lays*,
And holy *Orpheus*, Nature's *busy* child,
By headlong *Hebrus* his deep *hymns* compil'd;
Soft *Petrarch* – thaw'd by *Laura's* flames – did weep
On *Tiber's* banks, when she – *proud fair!* – could sleep;
Mosella boasts *Ausonius*, and the *Thames*
Doth murmur *Sidney's Stell*a to her *streams*;
While *Severn*, swoln with *joy* and *sorrow*, wears
Castara's smiles mix'd with fair *Sabrin's* tears.
Thus *poets* – like the *nymphs*, their *pleasing themes* –
Haunted the *bubbling springs* and *gliding streams*;
And *happy banks*! whence such *fair flow'rs* have
                                    sprung,
But happier those where they have *sat* and *sung*!
Poets – like *angels* – where they once appear
Hallow the *place*, and each succeeding year
Adds *rev'rence* to't, such as at length doth give
This aged faith, *that there their genii live.*
Hence th' *ancients* say, that from this *sickly air*
They pass to *regions* more *refin'd* and *fair*,
To *meadows* strew'd with *lilies* and the *rose*,
And *shades* whose *youthful green* no *old age* knows;
Where all in *white* they walk, discourse, and sing
Like bees' *soft murmurs*, or a *chiding spring*.
    But *Isca*, whensoe'er those *shades* I see,
And thy *lov'd arbours* must no more *know* me,
When I am laid to *rest* hard by thy *streams*,

And my *sun sets*, where first it *sprang* in beams,
I'll leave behind me such a *large, kind light*,
As shall *redeem* thee from *oblivious* night,
And in these *vows* which – living yet – I pay,
Shed such a *previous* and *enduring ray*,
As shall from age to age thy *fair name* lead,
'Till *rivers* leave to *run*, and *men* to *read*.
First, may all *bards* born after me
 – When I am *ashes* – sing of thee!
May thy *green banks* or *streams*, – or none –
Be both their *hill* and *Helicon*!
May *vocal groves* grow there, and all
The *shades* in them *prophetical*,
Where laid men shall more *fair truths* see
Than *fictions* were of *Thessaly*!
May thy gentle *swains* – like *flow'rs* –
Sweetly spend their *youthful hours*,
And thy *beauteous nymphs* – like *doves* –
Be *kind* and *faithful* to their *loves*!
Garlands, and *songs*, and *roundelays*,
Mild, dewy *nights*, and sunshine *days*,
The t*urtle's voice, joy* without *fear*,
Dwell on thy *bosom* all the year!
May the *evet* and the *toad*
Within thy banks have no abode,
Nor the *wily, winding snake*
Her *voyage* through thy *waters* make!
In all thy *journey* to the *main*
No *nitrous clay*, nor *brimstone-vein*
Mix with thy *streams*, but may they pass
Fresh on the *air*, and clear as *glass*,
And where the *wand'ring crystal* treads

Roses shall *kiss*, and *couple* heads!
The *factor-wind* from far shall bring
The *odours* of the *scatter'd* Spring,
And *loaden* with the rich *arrear*,
Spend it in *spicy whispers* there.
No *sullen heats*, nor *flames* that are
Offensive, and *canicular*,
Shine on thy *sands*, nor *pry* to see
Thy *scaly, shading family*,
But *noons* as mild as *Hesper's* rays,
Or the first *blushes* of fair days!
What *gifts* more *Heav'n* or *Earth* can add,
With all those *blessings* be thou *clad*!
    Honour, Beauty,
    Faith and *Duty*,
    Delight and *Truth*,
    With *Love* and *Youth*,
Crown all about thee! and whatever *Fate*
Impose elsewhere, whether the graver state
Or some toy else, may those *loud, anxious* cares
For *dead* and *dying things* – the common wares
And *shows* of Time – ne'er break thy *peace*, nor make
Thy *repos'd* arms to a new war *awake*!
    But *freedom*, *safety*, *joy* and *bliss*,
    United in one loving *kiss*,
    Surround thee quite, and *style* thy borders
   The land redeem'd from all disorders!

A Fluvium Iscam

Isca parens florum, placido qui spumens ore
    Lambis lapillos aureos,
Qui maestos hyacinthos, et picti tophi
    Mulces susurris humidis,
Dumque novas pergunt menses consumere lunas
    Coelumque mortales terit,
Accumulas cum sole dies, aevumque per omne
    Fidelis induras latex,
O quis inaccessos et quali murmure lucos
    Mutumque solaris nemus!
Per te discerpti credo Thracis ire querelas
Plectrumque divini sensis.

To the River Usk

Usk, father of flowers, foaming from your quiet spring,
you lap the golden pebbles, and with your moist
murmurings soothe the sorrowful hyacinths and the
flora on the colourful rock; and while the months run
on to engulf new moons, and heaven wears down
mortal men, you number your days with the sun, and
last out every age, an unfailing stream. What comfort
you bring to the remote woods and the silent grove, and
with what a murmurous whisper! I believe that the
plaints of the dismembered Thracian move along your
waters, and the lyre of the divine old man.

An Epitaph Upon the Lady Elizabeth, Second Daughter to His Late Majesty

Youth, Beauty, Virtue, Innocence
Heaven's royal, and select expense,
With virgin-tears, and sighs divine,
Sit here the *genii* of this shrine,
Where now (thy fair soul winged away,)
They guard the casket where she lay.
   Thou hadst, ere thou the light couldst see,
Sorrows laid up, and stored for thee,
Thou suck'dst in woes, and the *breasts* lent
Their *milk* to thee, but to lament;
Thy portion here was *grief*, thy years
Distilled no other rain, but tears,
Tears without noise, but (understood)
As loud, and shrill as any blood;
Thou seem'st a *rose-bud* born in *snow*,
A flower of purpose sprung to bow
To headless tempests, and the rage
Of an incensed, stormy age.
Others, ere their afflictions grow,
Are timed, and seasoned for the blow,
But thine, as *rheums* the tenderest part,
Fell on a *young* and *harmless* heart.
And yet as *balm-trees* gently spend
Their tears for those, that do them rend,
So mild and pious thou wert seen,
Though full of *sufferings,* free from *spleen,*
Thou didst nor murmur, nor revile,

But drank'st thy *wormwood* with a *smile*,
As envious eyes blast, and infect
And cause misfortunes by aspect,
So thy sad stars dispensed to thee
No influx, but calamity,
They viewed thee with *eclipsed* rays,
And but the *back-side* of bright days.

•   •   •

These were the comforts she had here,
As by an unseen hand 'tis clear,
Which now she reads, and smiling wears
A crown with him, who wipes off tears.

To My Worthy Friend, Master T. Lewes

Sees not my friend, what a deep snow
Candies our country's woody brow?
The yielding branch his load scarce bears
Oppressed with snow, and *frozen tears*,
While the *dumb* rivers slowly float,
All bound up in an *icy coat*.
　　Let us meet then! and while this world
In wild *eccentrics* now is hurled,
Keep we, like nature, the same *key*,
And walk in our forefathers' way;
Why any more cast we an eye
On what *may come*, not what is *nigh*?
Why vex our selves with *fear*, or *hope*
And cares beyond our *horoscope*?
Who into future times would peer
Looks oft beyond his term set here,
And cannot go into those grounds
But through a *church-yard* which them bounds;
Sorrows and sighs and searches spend
And draw our bottom to an end,
But discreet joys lengthen the lease
Without which life were a disease,
And who this age a mourner goes,
Doth with his tears but feed his foes.

To My Worthy Friend, Mr Henry Vaughan the Silurist

See what thou wert! by what Platonic round
Art thou in thy first youth and glories found?
Or from thy Muse does this retrieve accrue?
Does she which once inspir'd thee, now renew,
Bringing thee back those golden years which Time
Smooth'd to thy lays, and polish'd with thy rhyme?
Nor is't to thee alone she does convey
Such happy change, but bountiful as day,
On whatsoever reader she does shine,
She makes him like thee, and for ever thine.
And first thy manual op'ning gives to see
Eclipse and suff'rings burnish majesty,
Where thou so artfully the draught hast made
That we best read the lustre in the shade,
And find our sov'reign greater in that shroud:
So lightning dazzles from its night and cloud,
So the *First Light Himself* has for His throne
Blackness, and darkness his pavilion.
Who can refuse thee company, or stay,
By thy next charming summons forc'd away,
If that be force which we can so resent,
That only in its joys 'tis violent:
Upward thy *Eagle* bears us ere aware,
Till above storms and all tempestuous air
We radiant worlds with their bright people meet,
Leaving this little *all* beneath our feet.
But now the pleasure is too great to tell,

Nor have we other bus'ness than to dwell,
As on the hallow'd Mount th' Apostles meant
To build and fix their glorious banishment.
Yet we must know and find thy skilful vein
Shall gently bear us to our homes again;
By which descent thy former flight's impli'd
To be thy ecstacy and not thy pride.
And here how well does the wise *Muse* demean
Herself, and fit her song to ev'ry scene!
Riot of courts, the bloody wreaths of war,
Cheats of the mart, and clamours of the bar,
Nay, life itself thou dost so well express,
Its hollow joys, and real emptiness,
That *Dorian* minstrel never did excite,
Or raise for dying so much appetite.

Nor does thy other softer magic move
Us less thy fam'd *Etesia* to love;
Where such a *character* thou giv'st, that shame
Nor envy dare approach the vestal dame:
So at bright prime *ideas* none repine,
They safely in th' *eternal poet* shine.

Gladly th' *Assyrian phœnix* now resumes
From thee this last reprisal of his plumes;
He seems another more miraculous thing,
Brighter of crest, and stronger of his wing,
Proof against Fate in spicy urns to come,
Immortal past all risk of martyrdom.

Nor be concern'd, nor fancy thou art rude
T' adventure from thy Cambrian solitude:

Best from those lofty cliffs thy *Muse* does spring
Upwards, and boldly spreads her cherub wing.
So when the *sage* of *Memphis* would converse
With boding skies, and th' azure universe,
He climbs his starry pyramid, and thence
Freely sucks clean prophetic influence,
And all serene, and rapt and gay he pries
Through the ethereal volume's mysteries,
Loth to come down, or ever to know more
The *Nile's* luxurious, but dull foggy shore.

I. W., A.M. Oxon.

To the Most Excellently Accomplished, Mrs K. Philips

Say, witty fair one, from what sphere
Flow these rich numbers you shed here?
For sure such *incantations* come
From thence, which strike your readers dumb.
A strain, whose measures gently meet
Like *virgin-lovers* or Time's *feet*;
Where language *smiles*, and accents rise
As quick and pleasing as your *eyes*;
The *poem* smooth, and in each line
Soft as *yourself*, yet *masculine*;
Where not coarse trifles blot the page
With matter borrow'd from the age,
But thoughts as innocent and high
As *angels* have, or *saints* that die.
    These raptures when I first did see
New miracles in poetry,
And by a hand their good would miss
His *bays* and *fountains* but to kiss,
My weaker *genius* – cross to fashion –
Slept in a silent admiration:
A rescue, by whose grave disguise
Pretenders oft have pass'd for wise.
And yet as *pilgrims* humbly touch
Those *shrines* to which they bow so much,
And clouds in courtship flock, and run
To be the mask unto the sun,
So I concluded it was true

I might at distance worship you,
A *Persian* votary, and say
It was your light show'd me the way.
So *loadstones* guide the duller *steel*,
And high perfections are the *wheel*
Which moves the less, for gifts divine
Are strung upon a *vital line*,
Which, touch'd by you, excites in all
Affections *epidemical*.
And this made me – a truth most fit –
Add my weak *echo* to your wit;
Which pardon, Lady, for assays
Obscure as these might blast your bays;
As common hands soil *flow'rs*, and make
That dew they wear *weep* the mistake.
But I'll wash off the *stain*, and vow
No *laurel* grows but for your *brow*.

Song

Amyntas *go, thou art undone,*
  Thy faithful heart is cross'd by fate;
That love is better not begun,
  Where love is come to love too late.[43]
Had she professèd[44] hidden fires,
  Or show'd one[45] knot that tied her heart,
I could have quench'd my first desires,
  And we had only met to part.
But, tyrant, thus to murder men,
  And shed a lover's harmless blood,
And burn him in those flames again,
  Which he at first might have withstood.
Yet, who that saw fair Chloris *weep*
  Such sacred dew, with such pure[46] grace;
Durst think them feignèd tears, or seek
  For treason in an angel's face.
This is her art, though this be true,
  Men's joys are kill'd with[47] griefs and fears,
Yet she, like flowers oppress'd with dew,
  Doth thrive and flourish in her tears.

To Amoret, The Sigh

Nimble sigh, on thy warm wings,
    Take this message and depart;
Tell *Amoret*, that smiles and sings,
At what thy airy voyage brings,
    That thou cam'st lately from my heart.

Tell my lovely foe that I
    Have no more such spies to send,
But one or two that I intend,
Some few minutes ere I die,
    To her white bosom to commend.

Then whisper by that holy spring,
    Where for her sake I would have died,
Whilst those water-nymphs did bring
    Flowers to cure what she had tried;
And of my faith and love did sing.

That if my *Amoret*, if she
    In after-times would have it read,
How her beauty murder'd me,
With all my heart I will agree,
    If she'll but love me, being dead.

To Amoret, Walking in a Starry Evening

If *Amoret*, that glorious eye,
    In the first birth of light,
    And death of night,
Had with those elder fires you spy
    Scattered so high
    Received form, and sight;

We might suspect in the vast Ring,
    Amidst these golden glories,
    And fiery stories;
Whether the Sun had been the King,
    And guide of Day,
    Or your brighter eye should sway;

But, *Amoret,* such is my fate,
    That if thy face a Star
    Had shined from far,
I am persuaded in that state
    'Twixt thee, and me,
    Of some predestined sympathy.

For sure such two conspiring minds,
    Which no accident, or sight,
    Did thus unite;
Whom no distance can confine,

Start, or decline,
One, for another, were designed.

To Amoret, of the Difference 'Twixt Him, and Other Lovers, and What True Love Is

Mark, when the evening's cooler wings
   Fan the afflicted air, how the faint sun,
     Leaving undone,
     What he begun,
Those spurious flames suck'd up from slime and earth
     To their first, low birth,
     Resigns, and brings.

They shoot their tinsel beams and vanities,
   Threading with those false fires their way;
     But as you stay
     And see them stray,
You lose the flaming track, and subtly they
     Languish away,
     And cheat your eyes.

Just so base, sublunary lovers' hearts
   Fed on loose profane desires,
     May for an eye
     Or face comply:
But those remov'd, they will as soon depart,
     And show their art,
     And painted fires.

To Amoret Weeping

Leave, *Amoret*, melt not away so fast
Thy eyes' fair treasure; Fortune's wealthiest cast
Deserves not one such pearl; for these, well spent,
Can purchase stars, and buy a tenement
For us in heaven; though here the pious streams
Avail us not; who from that clue of sunbeams
Could ever steal one thread? or with a kind
Persuasive accent charm the wild loud wind?
    Fate cuts us all in marble, and the Book
Forestalls our glass of minutes; we may look
But seldom meet a change; think you a tear
Can blot the flinty volume? shall our fear
Or grief add to their triumphs? and must we
Give an advantage to adversity?
Dear, idle prodigal! is it not just
We bear our stars? What though I had not dust
Enough to cabinet a worm? nor stand
Enslav'd unto a little dirt, or sand?
I boast a better purchase, and can show
The glories of a soul that's simply true.
    But grant some richer planet at my birth
Had spied me out, and measur'd so much earth
Or gold unto my share: I should have been
Slave to these lower elements, and seen
My high-born soul flag with their dross, and lie
A pris'ner to base mud, and alchemy.
I should perhaps eat orphans, and suck up
A dozen distress'd widows in one cup;

Nay, further, I should by that lawful stealth,
Damn'd usury, undo the commonwealth;
Or patent it in soap, and coals, and so
Have the smiths curse me, and my laundress too;
Geld wine, or his friend tobacco; and so bring
The incens'd subject rebel to his king;
And after all – as those first sinners fell –
Sink lower than my gold, and lie in hell.
    Thanks then for this deliv'rance! blessed pow'rs,
You that dispense man's fortune and his hours,
How am I to you all engag'd! that thus
By such strange means, almost miraculous,
You should preserve me; you have gone the way
To make me rich by taking all away.
For I – had I been rich – as sure as fate,
Would have been meddling with the king, or State,
Or something to undo me; and 'tis fit,
We know, that who hath wealth should have no wit,
But, above all, thanks to that Providence
That arm'd me with a gallant soul, and sense,
'Gainst all misfortunes, that hath breath'd so much
Of Heav'n into me, that I scorn the touch
Of these low things; and can with courage dare
Whatever fate or malice can prepare:
I envy no man's purse or mines: I know
That, losing them, I've lost their curses too;
And *Amoret* – although our share in these
Is not contemptible, nor doth much please –
Yet, whilst content and love we jointly vie,
    We have a blessing which no gold can buy.

Les Amours

Tyrant farewell: this heart, the prize
And triumph of thy scornful eyes,
I sacrifice to heaven, and give
To quit my sins, that durst believe
A woman's easy faith, and place
True joys in a changing face.
   Yet ere I go; by all those tears,
And sighs I spent 'twixt hopes, and fears;
By thy own glories, and that hour
Which first enslaved me to thy power;
I beg, fair one, by this last breath,
This tribute from thee after death.
If when I'm gone, you chance to see
That cold bed where I lodged be:
Let not your hate in death appear,
But bless my ashes with a tear:
This influx from that quickening eye,
By secret power, which none can spy,
The cold dust shall inform, and make
Those flames (though dead) new life partake.
Whose warmth helped by your tears shall bring,
O'er all the tomb a sudden spring
Of crimson flowers, whose drooping heads
Shall curtain o'er their mournful beds:
And on each leaf by Heaven's command,
These emblems to the life shall stand:
   Two hearts, the first a shaft withstood;
The second, shot, and washed in blood;

And on this heart a dew shall stay,
Which no heat can court away;
But fixed for ever witness bears,
That hearty sorrow feeds on tears.
    Thus Heaven can make it known, and true,
    That you killed me, 'cause I loved you.

To His Friend, Being In Love

Ask, lover, ere thou diest; let one poor breath
Steal from thy lips, to tell her of thy death;
Doating idolater! can silence bring
Thy saint propitious? or will *Cupid* fling
One arrow for thy paleness? leave to try
This silent courtship of a sickly eye.
Witty to tyranny, she too well knows
This but the incense of thy private vows,
That breaks forth at thine eyes, and doth betray
The sacrifice thy wounded heart would pay;
Ask her, fool, ask her; if words cannot move,
The language of thy tears may make her love.

   Flow nimbly from me then; and when you fall
On her breast's warmer snow, O may you all,
By some strange fate fix'd there, distinctly lie,
The much lov'd volume of my tragedy.

   Where, if you win her not, may this be read,
The cold that freez'd you so, did strike me dead.

An Elegy

'Tis true, I am undone: yet, ere I die,
I'll leave these sighs and tears a legacy
To after-lovers: that, rememb'ring me,
Those sickly flames which now benighted be,
Fann'd by their warmer sighs, may love; and prove
In them the metempsychosis of love.
'Twas I – when others scorn'd – vow'd you were fair,
And sware that breath enrich'd the coarser air,
Lent roses to your cheeks, made Flora bring
Her nymphs with all the glories of the spring
To wait upon thy face, and gave my heart
A pledge to *Cupid* for a quicker dart,
To arm those eyes against myself; to me
Thou ow'st that tongue's bewitching harmony.
I courted angels from those upper joys,
And made them leave their spheres to hear thy voice.
I made the Indian curse the hours he spent
To seek his pearls, and wisely to repent
His former folly, and confess a sin,
Charm'd by the brighter lustre of thy skin.
I borrow'd from the winds the gentler wing
Of *Zephyrus*, and soft souls of the spring;
And made – to air those cheeks with fresher grace –
The warm inspirers dwell upon thy face.

Oh! jam satis

✳ *196*

The Charnel-House

Bless me! what damps are here! how stiff an air!
Kelder of mists, a second *fiat's* care,
Front'spiece o' th' grave and darkness, a display
Of ruin'd man, and the disease of day,
Lean, bloodless shamble, where I can descry
Fragments of men, rags of anatomy,
Corruption's wardrobe, the transplantive bed
Of mankind, and th' exchequer of the dead!
How thou arrests my sense! how with the sight
My *winter'd* blood grows stiff to all delight!
Torpedo to the eye! whose least glance can
Freeze our wild lusts, and rescue headlong man.
Eloquent silence! able to immure
An *atheist's* thoughts, and blast an *epicure.*
Were I a *Lucian*, Nature in this dress
Would make me wish a Saviour, and confess.
   Where are you, shoreless thoughts, vast tenter'd
                        hope,
Ambitious dreams, *aims* of an endless scope,
Whose stretch'd excess runs on a string too high,
And on the rack of self-extension die?
Chameleons of state, air-monging band,
Whose breath – like gunpowder – blows up a land,
Come see your dissolution, and weigh
What a loath'd nothing you shall be one day.
As th' elements by circulation pass
From one to th' other, and that which first was
I so again, so 'tis with you; the grave

And Nature but complot; what the one gave
The other takes; think, then, that in this bed
There sleep the relics of as proud a head,
As stern and subtle as your own, that hath
Perform'd, or forc'd as much, whose tempest-wrath
Hath levell'd kings with slaves, and wisely then
Calm these high furies, and descend to men.
Thus *Cyrus* tam'd the *Macedon*; a tomb
Check'd him, who thought the world too straight a
                                           room.
    Have I obey'd the *powers* of face,
A beauty able to undo the race
Of easy man? I look but here, and straight
I am inform'd, the lovely counterfeit
Was but a smoother clay. That famish'd slave
Beggar'd by wealth, who starves that he may save,
Brings hither but his sheet; nay, th' *ostrich-man*
That feeds on *steel* and *bullet*, he that can
Outswear his *lordship*, and reply as tough
To a kind word, as if his tongue were *buff*,
Is *chap*-fall'n here: worms without wit or fear
Defy him now; Death hath disarm'd the *bear*.
Thus could I run o'er all the piteous score
Of erring men, and having done, meet more,
Their shuffled *wills*, abortive, vain *intents*,
Fantastic *humours*, perilous *ascents*,
False, empty *honours*, traitorous *delights*,
And whatsoe'er a blind conceit invites;
But these and more which the weak vermins swell,
Are couch'd in this accumulative cell,
Which I could scatter; but the grudging sun
Calls home his beams, and warns me to be gone;

* *198*

Day leaves me in a double night, and I
Must bid farewell to my sad library.
Yet with these notes – Henceforth with thought of thee
I'll season all succeeding jollity,
Yet damn not mirth, nor think too much is fit;
Excess hath no *religion*, nor *wit*;
But should wild blood swell to a lawless strain,
One check from thee shall *channel* it again.

A Rhapsody

*Occasionally written upon a meeting with some of his
friends at the Globe Tavern, in a chamber painted
overhead with a cloudy sky and some few dispersed
stars, and on the sides with landscapes, hills,
shepherds and sheep.*

Darkness, and stars i's th' mid-day! They invite
Our active fancies to believe it night:
For taverns need no sun, but for a sign,
Where rich tobacco and quick tapers shine;
And royal, witty sack, the poet's soul,
With brighter suns than he doth gild the bowl;
As though the pot and poet did agree,
Sack should to both illuminator be.
That artificial cloud, with its curl'd brow,
Tells us 'tis late; and that blue space below
Is fir'd with many stars: mark! how they break
In silent glances o'er the hills, and speak
The evening to the plains, where, shot from far,
They meet in dumb salutes, as one great star.
    The room, methinks, grows darker; and the air
Contracts a sadder colour, and less fair.
Or is't the drawer's skill? hath he no arts
To blind us so we can't know pints from quarts?
No, no, 'tis night: look where the jolly clown
Musters his bleating herd and quits the down.

Hark! how his rude pipe frets the quiet air,
Whilst ev'ry hill proclaims *Lycoris* fair.
Rich, happy man! that canst thus watch and sleep,
Free from all cares, but thy wench, pipe and sheep!
    But see, the moon is up; view, where she stands
Sentinel o'er the door, drawn by the hands
Of some base painter, that for gain hath made
Her face the landmark to the tippling trade.
This cup to her, that to *Endymion* give;
'Twas wit at first, and wine that made them live.
Choke may the painter! and his box disclose
No other colours than his fiery nose;
And may we no more of his pencil see
Than two churchwardens, and mortality.
    Should we go now a-wand'ring, we should meet
With catchpoles, whores and carts in ev'ry street:
Now when each narrow lane, each nook and cave,
Sign-posts and shop-doors, pimp for ev'ry knave,
When riotous sinful plush, and tell-tale spurs
Walk Fleet Street and the Strand, when the soft stirs
Of bawdy, ruffled silks, turn night to day;
And the loud whip and coach scolds all the way;
When lust of all sorts, and each itchy blood
From the Tower-wharf to Cymbeline, and Lud,
Hunts for a mate, and the tir'd footman reels
'Twixt chairmen, torches, and the hackney wheels.
    Come, take the other dish; it is to him
That made his horse a senator: each brim
Look big as mine: the gallant, jolly beast
Of all the herd – you'll say – was not the least.
Now crown the second bowl, rich as his worth
I'll drink it to; he, that like fire broke forth

Into the Senate's face, cross'd Rubicon,
And the State's pillars, with their laws thereon,
And made the dull grey beards and furr'd gowns fly
Into *Brundusium* to consult, and lie.
    This, to brave *Sylla!* why should it be said
We drink more to the living than the dead?
Flatt'rers and fools do use it: let us laugh
At our own honest mirth; for they that quaff
To honour others, do like those that sent
Their gold and plate to strangers to be spent.
    Drink deep; this cup be pregnant, and the wine
Spirit of wit, to make us all divine,
That big with sack and mirth we may retire
Possessors of more souls, and nobler fire;
And by the influx of this painted sky,
And labour'd forms, to higher matters fly;
So, if a nap shall take us, we shall all,
    After full cups, have dreams poetical.

Let's laugh now, and the press'd grape drink,
Till the drowsy day-star wink;
And in our merry, mad mirth run
Faster, and further than the sun;
And let none his cup forsake,
Till that star again doth wake;
So we men below shall move
Equally with the gods above.

Fida: Or the Country Beauty: to Lysimachus

Now I have seen her; and by *Cupid*
The young *Medusa* made me stupid!
A face, that hath no lovers slain,
Wants forces, and is near disdain.
For every *fop* will freely peep
At majesty that is asleep.
But she (fair tyrant!) hates to be
Gazed on with such impunity.
Whose prudent rigour bravely bears
And scorns the trick of whining tears:
Or sighs, those false alarms of grief,
Which kill not, but afford relief.
Nor is it thy hard fate to be
Alone in this calamity,
Since I who came but to be gone,
Am plagued for merely looking on.

    Mark from her forehead to her foot
What charming *sweets* are there to do't.
A *head* adorned with all those glories
That *wit* hath shadowed in quaint stories:
Or *pencil* with rich colours drew
In imitation of the true.

    Her *hair* laid out in curious *sets*
And *twists*, doth show like silken *nets*,
Where (since he played at *hit* or *miss*:)
The God of *Love* her prisoner is,
And fluttering with his skittish wings

Puts all her locks in curls and rings.
  Like twinkling stars her *eyes* invite
All gazers to so sweet a light,
But then two *arched clouds* of brown
Stand o'er, and guard them with a frown.
  Beneath these rays of her bright eyes
Beauty's rich *bed* of *blushes* lies.
Blushes, which lightning-like come on,
Yet stay not to be gazed upon;
But leave the *lilies* of her skin
As fair as ever, and run in:
Like swift *salutes* (which dull *paint* scorn,)
Twixt a *white* noon, and *crimson* morn.
  What *coral* can her *lips* resemble?
For hers are warm, swell, melt and tremble:
And if you dare contend for *red*,
This is *alive*, the other *dead.*
  Her equal *teeth* (above, below:)
All of a size, and *smoothness* grow.
Where under close restraint and awe
(Which is the maiden, tyrant law:)
Like a caged, sullen *linnet*, dwells
Her *tongue*, the *key* to potent spells.
  Her *skin*, like heaven when calm and bright,
Shows a rich *azure* under *white*,
With *touch* more soft than heart supposes,
And *breath* as sweet as new blown *roses.*
  Betwixt this *head-land* and the *main*,
Which is a rich and flowery *plain*:
Lies her fair *neck*, so fine and slender
That (gently) how you please, 'twill bend her.
  This leads you to her *heart*, which ta'en

Pants under *sheets* of whitest *lawn*,
And at the first seems much distressed,
But nobly treated, lies at rest.
　　Here like two *balls* of new fallen snow,
Her *breasts*, Love's native *pillows* grow;
And out of each a *rose-bud* peeps
Which *infant* beauty sucking, sleeps.
　　Say now my *Stoic*, that mak'st sour faces
At all the *Beauties* and the *Graces*,
That criest *unclean!* though known thy self
To every coarse, and dirty shelf:
Coulst thou but see a *piece* like this,
A piece so full of *sweets* and *bliss*:
In *shape* so rare, in *soul* so rich,
Wouldst thou not swear she is a witch?

To Etesia (for Timander), the First Sight

What smiling *star* in that fair night
Which gave you *birth* gave me this *sight*,
And with a kind *aspect* tho' keen
Made me the *subject*, you the *queen*?
That sparkling *planet* is got now
Into your eyes, and shines below,
Where nearer force and more acute
It doth dispense, without dispute;
For I who yesterday did know
Love's fire no more than doth cool snow,
With one bright look am since undone,
Yet must adore and seek my sun.
   Before I walk'd free as the wind
And if but stay'd – like it – unkind;
I could like daring eagles gaze
And not be blinded by a face;
For what I saw till I saw thee,
Was only not deformity.
Such shapes appear – compar'd with thine –
In *arras*, or a tavern-sign,
And do but mind me to explore
A fairer piece, that is in store.
So some hang *ivy* to their wine,
To signify there is a *vine*.
   Those princely flow'rs – by no storms vex'd –
Which smile one day, and droop the next,
The gallant *tulip* and the *rose*,

Emblems which some use to disclose
Bodied *ideas* – their weak grace
Is mere imposture to thy face.
For Nature in all things, but thee,
Did practise only *sophistry*;
Or else she made them to express
How she could vary in her dress:
But thou wert form'd, that we might see
Perfection, not variety.

Have you observ'd how the day-star
Sparkles and smiles and shines from far;
Then to the gazer doth convey
A silent but a piercing ray?
So wounds my love, but that her eyes
Are in *effects* the better skies.
A brisk bright *agent* from them streams
Arm'd with no arrows, but their beams,
And with such stillness smites our hearts,
No noise betrays him, nor his darts.
He, working on my easy soul,
Did soon persuade, and then control;
And now he flies – and I conspire –
Through all my blood with wings of fire,
And when I would – which will be never –
With cold despair allay the fever,
The spiteful thing *Etesia* names,
And that new-fuels all my flames.

The Character, to Etesia

Go catch the *phoenix*, and then bring
A *quill* drawn for me from his wing.
Give me a maiden-beauty's *blood*,
A pure, rich *crimson*, without mud:
In whose sweet *blushes* that may live,
Which a dull verse can never give.
Now for an untouched, spotless *white*,
For blackest things on paper write;
Etesia at thine own expense
Give me the *robes* of innocence.

   Could we but see a *spring* to run
Pure *milk*, as sometimes springs have done,
And in the *snow-white* streams it sheds
Carnations wash their *bloody* heads.
While every *eddy* that came down
Did (as thou dost,) both *smile* and *frown*.
Such objects and so fresh would be
But dull resemblance of thee.

   Thou art the dark world's morning-star,
Seen only, and seen but from far;
Where like astronomers we gaze
upon the glories of thy face,
But no acquaintance more can have,
Though all our lives we watch and crave.
Thou art a world thy self alone,
Yea three great worlds refined to one.
Which shows all those, and in thine eyes
The shining *east*, and *Paradise*.

Thy soul (a *spark* of the first *fire*,)
Is like the *sun*, the world's desire;
And with a nobler influence
Works upon all, that claim to sense;
But in *summers* hath no *fever*,
And in frosts is cheerful ever.

As *flowers*, besides their curious *dress*
Rich *odours* have, and *sweetnesses*,
Which tacitly infuse desire
And even oblige us to admire:
Such and so full of innocence
Are all the *charms*, thou dost dispense;
And like fair *nature*, without *arts*
At once they seize, and please our hearts.
O thou art such, that I could be
A lover to idolatry!
I could, and should from heaven stray,
But that thy life shows mine the way,
And leave a while the *Deity*,
To serve his *image* here in thee.

To Etesia Looking From Her Casement at the Full Moon

See you that beauteous *Queen*, which no age tames?
Her train is *azure*, set with *golden* flames.
My brighter *fair*, fix on the *east* your eyes,
And view that bed of clouds, whence she doth rise.
Above all others in that one short hour
Which most concerned me, she had greatest power.
This made my *fortunes* humorous as wind,
But fixed *affections* to my constant mind.
She fed me with the *tears* of *stars*, and thence
I sucked in *sorrows* with their *influence*.
To some in *smiles*, and store of *light* she broke:
To me in sad *eclipses* still she spoke.
She bent me with the motion of her *sphere*,
And made me feel, what first I did but ear.
    But when I came to age, and had o'ergrown
Her rules, and saw my freedom was my own,
I did reply unto the laws of fate,
And made my reason, my great advocate:
I laboured to inherit my just right;
But then (O hear *Etesia*!) lest I might
Redeem my self, my unkind Starry mother
Took my poor heart, and gave it to another.

To Etesia Parted From Him, and Looking Back

O, subtle Love! thy peace is war,
It wounds and kills without a scar,
It works unknown to any sense,
Like the decrees of Providence,
And with strange silence shoots me through,
The *fire* of Love doth fell like *snow*.
   Hath she no *quiver*, but my heart?
Must all her arrows hit that part?
Beauties like heav'n their gifts should deal
Not to destroy us, but to heal.
Strange *art* of Love! that can make sound,
And yet exasperates the wound:
That *look* she lent to ease my heart,
Hath pierc'd it, and improv'd the smart.

To Etesia Going Beyond Sea

Go, if you must! but stay – and know
And mind before you go, my vow.
    To every thing, but *Heaven* and *you*,
With all my heart, I bid adieu!
Now to those happy *shades* I'll go
Where first I saw my beauteous foe.
I'll seek each silent *path*, where we
Did walk, and where you sat with me
I'll sit again, and never rest
Till I can find some *flower* you pressed.
That near my dying heart I'll keep,
And when it wants *dew*, I will weep:
Sadly I will repeat past joys,
And words, which you did sometimes voice:
I'll listen to the *woods*, and hear
The *Echo* answer for you there.
But famished with long absence I
Like *infants* left, at last shall cry,
And tears (as they do *milk*) will sup
Until you come, and take me up.

Etesia Absent

Love, the world's life! what a sad death
Thy absence is! to lose our breath
At once and die, is but to live
Enlarg'd, without the scant reprieve
Of *pulse* and *air*; whose dull *returns*
And narrow *circles* the soul mourns.
   But to be dead alive, and still
To wish, but never have our will,
To be possess'd, and yet to miss,
To wed a true but absent bliss,
Are ling'ring tortures, and their smart
Dissects and racks and grinds the heart!
As soul and body in that state
Which unto us, seems separate,
Cannot be said to live, until
Reunion; which days fulfil
And slow-pac'd seasons; so in vain
Through hours and minutes – Time's long *train* –
I look for thee, and from thy sight,
As from my soul, for life and light.
For till thine eyes shine so on me,
Mine are fast-clos'd and will not see.

To His Books

Bright books! the *perspectives* to our weak sights:
The clear *projections* of discerning lights.
Burning and shining *thoughts*; man's posthume *day*:
The *track* of fled souls, and their *Milky-Way*.
The dead *alive* and *busy*, the still *voice*
Of enlarged spirits, kind heaven's white *decoys*.
Who lives with you, lives like those knowing *flowers*,
Which in commerce with *light*, spend all their hours:
Which shut to *clouds*, and *shadows* nicely shun;
But with glad haste unveil to *kiss* the sun.
Beneath you all is dark and a dead night;
Which whoso lives in, wants both health and sight.
    By sucking you, the wise (like *bees*) do grow
Healing and rich, though this they do most slow:
Because most choicely, for as great a store
Have we of *books*, as bees of *herbs*, or more.
And the great task to *try*, then know the good:
To discern *weeds,* and judge of wholesome *food*,
Is a rare, scant performance; for *man* dies
Oft ere 'tis done, while the *bee* feeds and flies.
But you were all choice *flowers*, all set and dressed
By old, sage *florists,* who well knew the best.
And I amidst you all am turned a *weed*!
Not wanting knowledge, but for want of heed.
Then thank thy self *wild fool*, that wouldst not be
Content to know – what was too much for thee!

*214

To Sir William Davenant, Upon His Gondibert

Well, we are rescued! and by thy rare pen
Poets shall live, when *princes* die like men.
Th' hast clear'd the prospect to our harmless *hill*,
Of late years clouded with imputed ill,
And the *soft, youthful couples* there may move,
As chaste as *stars* converse and smile above.
Th' hast taught their *language* and their *love* to flow
Calm as *rose-leaves*, and cool as *virgin-snow*,
Which doubly feasts us, being so refin'd,
They both *delight* and *dignify* the mind;
Like to the wat'ry music of some spring,
Whose pleasant flowings at once *wash* and *sing*.
    And where before *heroic poems* were
Made up of *spirits*, *prodigies*, and fear,
And show'd – through all the *melancholy flight* –
Like some dark region overcast with night,
As if the poet had been quite dismay'd,
While only *giants* and *enchantments* sway'd;
Thou like the *sun*, whose eye brooks no disguise,
Hast chas'd them hence, and with discoveries
So rare and learnèd fill'd the place, that we
Those fam'd *grandezas* find outdone by thee,
And underfoot see all those *vizards* hurl'd
Which bred the wonder of the former world.
'Twas dull to sit, as our forefathers did,
At *crumbs* and *voiders*, and because unbid,
Refrain wise appetite. This made thy *fire*

Break through the ashes of thy aged *sire*,
To lend the world such a convincing light
As shows his *fancy* darker than his sight.
Nor was't alone the *bars* and *length* of days
 - Though those gave *strength* and *stature* to his *bays* -
Encounter'd thee, but what's an old complaint
And kills the fancy, a *forlorn restraint*.
How couldst thou, mur'd in solitary stones,
Dress *Birtha's* smiles, though well thou mightst her
                                                    groans?
And, strangely eloquent, thyself divide
'Twixt *sad misfortunes* and a *bloomy bride*?
Through all the tenour of thy ample song,
Spun from thy own rich store, and shar'd among
Those fair *adventurers*, we plainly see
Th' *imputed* gifts *inherent* are in thee.
Then live for ever - and by high desert -
In thy own *mirror*, matchless *Gondibert*,
And in *bright Birtha* leave thy *love* enshrin'd
Fresh as her *em'rald*, and *fair* as her *mind*,
While all confess thee - as they ought to do -
The prince of *poets*, and of *lovers* too.

Distraction

O knit me, that am crumbled dust! the heap
  Is all dispersed, and cheap;
 Give for a handful, but a thought
   And it is bought;
    Hadst thou
Made me a star, a pearl, or a rain-bow,
  The beams I then had shot
  My light has lessened not,
    But now
I find my self the less, the more I grow;
    The world
Is full of voices; Man is called, and hurled
  By each, he answers all,
  Knows every note, and call,
    Hence, still
Fresh dotage tempts, or old usurps his will.
Yet, hadst thou clipped my wings, when confined in
  This quickened mass of sin,
 And saved that light, which freely thou
   Didst then bestow,
    I fear
I should have spurned, and said thou didst forbear;
  Or that thy store was less,
  But now since thou didst bless
    So much,
I grieve, my God! that thou hast made me such.
    I grieve?
O, yes! thou know'st I do; come, and relieve

217

And tame, and keep down with thy light
Dust that would rise, and dim my sight,
   Lest left alone too long
   Amidst the noise, and throng,
     Oppressed I
Striving to save the whole, by parcels die.

The Eagle

'Tis madness sure; and I am in the *fit*,
To dare an *eagle* with my *unfledg'd* wit.
For what did ever *Rome* or *Athens* sing
In all their *lines*, as lofty as his wing?
He that an eagle's *powers* would rehearse
Should with his plumes first feather all his verse.
　　I know not, when into thee I would pry,
Which to admire, thy *wing* first, or thine *eye*;
Or whether Nature at thy birth design'd
More of her *fire* for thee, or of her *wind*.
When thou in the clear *heights* and upmost *air*
Dost face the sun and his dispersèd hair,
Ev'n from that distance thou the *sea* dost spy
And sporting in its deep, wide lap, the *fry*.
Not the least *minnow* there but thou canst see:
Whole seas are narrow spectacles to thee.
　　Nor is this element of water here
Below of all thy miracles the sphere.
If poets ought may add unto thy store,
Thou hast in heav'n of wonders many more.
For when just *Jove* to earth his thunder bends,
And from that bright, eternal fortress sends
His louder volleys, straight this bird doth fly
To *Ætna*, where his magazine doth lie,
And in his active talons brings him more
Of ammunition, and recruits his store.
Nor is't a low or easy *lift*. He soars
'Bove *wind* and *fire*; gets to the *moon*, and pores

With scorn upon her duller face; for she
Gives him but shadows and obscurity.
Here much displeas'd, that anything like night
Should meet him in his proud and lofty flight,
That such dull *tinctures* should advance so far,
And rival in the glories of a star,
Resolv'd he is a nobler course to try,
And measures out his voyage with his eye.
Then with such fury he begins his flight,
As if his wings contended with his sight.
Leaving the moon, whose humble light doth trade
With *spots*, and deals most in the *dark* and *shade*,
To the day's royal *planet* he doth pass
With daring eyes, and makes the sun his glass.
Here doth he plume and dress himself, the beams
Rushing upon him like so many streams;
While with direct looks he doth entertain
The thronging flames, and shoots them back again.
And thus from star to star he doth repair,
And wantons in that pure and peaceful air.
Sometimes he frights the starry *swan*, and now
Orion's fearful *hare*, and then the crow.
Then with the *orb* itself he moves, to see
Which is more swift, th' *intelligence* or he.
Thus with his wings his body he hath brought
Where man can travel only in a thought.
   I will not seek, rare bird, what *spirit* 'tis
That mounts thee thus; I'll be content with this,
To think that Nature made thee to express
Our soul's bold *heights* in a material dress.

Midnight

I

When to my eyes
(Whilst deep sleep others catches,)
Thine host of spies
The stars shine in their watches,
I do survey
Each busy ray,
And how they work, and wind,
And wish each beam
My soul doth stream,
With the like ardour shined;
What emanations,
Quick vibrations
And bright stirs are there?
What thin ejections,
Cold affections,
And slow motions here?

2

   Thy heavens (some say,)
Are a fiery-liquid light,
   Which mingling aye
Streams, and flames thus to the sight.
   Come then, my god!
   Shine on this blood,
  And water in one beam,
   And thou shalt see
   Kindled by thee
Both liquors burn, and stream.
   O what bright quickness,
   Active brightness,
And celestial flows
   Will follow after
   On that water,
Which thy spirit blows!

Looking Back

Fair, shining *mountains* of my pilgrimage,
  And flowery *vales*, whose flowers were stars:
The *days* and *nights* of my first, happy age;
  An age without distaste and wars:
When I by thoughts ascend your *sunny heads*,
  And mind those sacred, *midnight* lights:
By which I walked, when curtained rooms and beds
  Confined, or sealed up others' sights:
    O then how bright
    And quick a light
  Doth brush my heart and scatter night;
    Chasing that shade
    Which my sins made,
  While I so *spring*, as if I could not *fade*!

How brave a prospect is a bright *back-side*!
  Where flowers and palms refresh the eye:
And days well spent like the glad *east* abide,
  Whose morning-glories cannot die!

The Shower

Waters above! eternal springs!
The dew that silvers the Dove's wings!
O welcome, welcome to the sad!
Give dry dust drink; drink that makes glad!
Many fair *ev'nings*, many *flow'rs*
Sweeten'd with rich and gentle showers,
Have I enjoy'd, and down have run
Many a fine and shining *sun*;
But never, till this happy hour,
Was blest with such an *evening-shower*!

Retirement

Fresh *fields* and woods! the Earth's fair *face*!
God's *footstool*! and man's *dwelling-place*!
I ask not why the first *believer*
Did love to be a country liver?
Who, to secure pious content,
Did pitch by *groves* and *wells* his tent;
Where he might view the boundless *sky*,
And all those glorious *lights* on high,
With flying *meteors*, *mists*, and *show'rs*,
Subjected *hills*, *trees*, *meads*, and *flow'rs*,
And ev'ry minute bless the King
And wise Creator of each thing.
   I ask not why he did remove
To happy *Mamre's* holy grove,
Leaving the *cities* of the plain
To *Lot* and his successless train?
All various lusts in *cities* still
Are found; they are the *thrones* of ill,
The dismal *sinks*, where blood is spill'd,
Cages with much uncleanness fill'd:
But *rural shades* are the sweet sense
Of piety and innocence;
They are the *meek's* calm region, where
Angels descend and rule the sphere;
Where Heaven lies *leiguer*, and the *Dove*
Duly as *dew* comes from above.
If *Eden* be on Earth at all,
'Tis that which we the *country* call.

The Day-Spring

Early, while yet the *dark* was gay
And *gilt* with stars, more trim than day,
Heav'n's *Lily*, and the Earth's chaste *Rose*,
The green immortal *Branch* arose;
And in a solitary place
Bow'd to His Father His blest face.
   If this calm season pleased my *Prince*,
Whose *fulness* no need could evince,
Why should not I, poor silly sheep,
His *hours*, as well as *practice*, keep?
Not that His hand is tied to these,
From whom *Time* holds his transient *lease*
But *mornings* new creations are,
When men, all night sav'd by His care,
Are still reviv'd; and well He may
Expect them grateful with the day.
So for that first *draught* of His hand,
Which finish'd heav'n, and sea, and land,
The *sons* of God their thanks did bring,
And all the *morning stars* did sing.
Besides, as His part heretofore
The *firstlings* were of all that bore
So now each day from all He saves
Their soul's *first thoughts* and fruits He craves.
This makes Him daily shed and show'r
His graces at this early hour;
Which both His care and kindness show,
Cheering the good, quickening the slow.

＊*228*

As holy friends mourn at delay,
And think each minute an hour's stay,
So His Divine and loving *Dove*
With longing throes[67] doth heave and move,
And soar about us while we sleep;
Sometimes quite through that *lock* doth *peep*,
And shine, but always without fail,
Before the slow sun can unveil,
In new *compassions* breaks, like light,
And *morning-looks*, which scatter night.
    And wilt Thou let Thy *creature* be,
When *Thou* hast watch'd, asleep to Thee?
Why to unwelcome loath'd surprises
Dost leave him, having left his vices?
Since these, if suffer'd, may again
Lead back the *living* to the *slain*.
O, change this *scourge*; or, if as yet
None less will my transgressions fit,
Dissolve, dissolve! Death cannot do
What I would not submit unto.

The Recovery

I

Fair *vessel* of our daily light, whose proud
And previous *glories* gild that blushing cloud;
Whose lively *fires* in swift projections glance
From hill to hill, and by refracted chance
Burnish some neighbour-*rock*, or tree, and then
Fly off in coy and wingèd *flames* again:
>   If thou this day
>   Hold on thy way,
Know, I have got a greater *light* than thine;
A light, whose *shade* and *back-parts* make thee shine.
>   Then get thee down! then get thee down!
>   I have a *Sun* now of my own.

II

Those nicer livers, who without thy rays
Stir not abroad, those may thy lustre praise;
And wanting light – *light*, which no *wants* doth know –
To thee – weak *shiner*! – like blind *Persians* bow.
But where that *Sun*, which tramples on thy head,
From His own bright eternal *eye* doth shed
>   One living *ray*,
>   There thy dead day
Is needless, and man to a *light* made free,
Which shows that thou canst neither show nor see.

* *230*

Then get thee down! then get thee down!
I have a *Sun* now of my own.

The Revival

Unfold, unfold! take in his light,
Who makes thy cares more short than night.
The joys, which with his *Day-star* rise,
He deals to all, but drowsy eyes:
And what the men of this world miss,
Some *drops* and *dews* of future bliss.
   Hark! how his *winds* have changed their *note*,
And with warm *whispers* call thee out.
The *frosts are past*, the *storms* are gone:
And backward *life* at last comes on.
The lofty *groves* in express joys
Reply unto the *turtle's* voice,
And here in *dust* and *dirt*, O here
The *lilies* of his love appear!

Regeneration

1

A ward, and still in bonds, one day
      I stole abroad,
It was high-spring, and all the way
      Primrosed, and hung with shade;
      Yet, was it frost within,
         And surly winds
Blasted my infant buds, and sin
      Like clouds eclipsed my mind.

2

Stormed thus, I straight perceived my spring
      Mere stage, and show,
My walk a monstrous, mountained thing
      Rough-cast with rocks, and snow;
      And as a pilgrim's eye
         Far from relief,
Measures the melancholy sky
      Then drops, and rains for grief,

3

So sighed I upwards still; at last
     'Twixt steps, and falls
I reached the pinnacle, where placed
     I found a pair of scales,
     I took them up and laid
      In the one late pains,
The other smoke, and pleasures weighed
     But proved the heavier grains;

4

With that, some cried, *Away*; straight I
     Obeyed, and led
Full east, a fair, fresh field could spy
     Some called it, *Jacob's bed*;
     A Virgin-soil, which no
      Rude feet ere trod,
Where (since he stepped there,) only go
     Prophets, and friends of God.

5

Here, I reposed; but scarce well set,
     A grove escried
Of stately height, whose branches met
     And mixed on every side;
     I entered, and once in
      (Amazed to see't,)

Found all was changed, and a new spring
    Did all my senses greet.

6

The unthrift Sun shot vital gold
    A thousand pieces,
And heaven its azure did unfold
    Chequered with snowy fleeces,
    The air was all in spice
    And every bush
A garland wore; thus fed my eyes
    But all the ear lay hush.

7

Only a little fountain lent
    Some use for ears,
And on the dumb shades language spent
    The music of her tears;
    I drew her near, and found
    The cistern full
Of divers stones, some bright, and round
    Others ill-shaped, and dull.

8

The first (pray mark,) as quick as light
      Danced through the flood,
But, the last more heavy than the night
      Nailed to the centre stood;
      I wondered much, but tired
        At last with thought,
My restless eye that still desired
    As strange an object brought;

9

It was a bank of flowers, where I descried
      (Though 'twas mid-day,)
Some fast asleep, others broad-eyed
      And taking in the ray,
      Here musing long, I heard
        A rushing wind
Which still increased, but whence it stirred
      No where I could not find;

10

I turned me round, and to each shade
      Dispatched an eye,
To see, if any leaf had made
      Least motion, or reply,
      But while I listening sought
        My mind to ease

By knowing, where 'twas, or where not,
    It whispered; *Where I please*

Lord, then said I, *On me one breath,*
And let me die before my death!

The World (II)

Can any tell me what it is? can you,
   That wind your thoughts into a *clue*
To guide out others, while your selves stay in,
           And hug the sin?
   I, who so long have in it lived,
      That if I might,
In truth I would not be reprieved:
      Have neither sight,
    Nor sense that knows
     These *ebbs* and *flows*.
But since of all, all may be said,
And *likeliness* doth but upbraid,
And mock the *truth*, which still is lost
In fine *conceits*, like streams in a sharp frost:
   I will not strive, nor the *rule* break
   Which doth give losers leave to speak.
Then false and foul World, and unknown
     Even to thy own:
Here I renounce thee, and resign
Whatever thou canst say, is thine.
   Thou art not *truth*; for he that tries
Shall find thee all deceit and lies.
Thou art not *friendship*; for in thee
'Tis but the *bait* of policy.
Which, like a *viper* lodged in *flowers*,
Its venom through that sweetness pours.
And when not so, then always 'tis
A fading *paint*; the short-lived bliss

Of *air* and *humour*: out and in
Like *colours* in a *dolphin's* skin.
But must not live beyond *one day*,
Or *convenience*; then away,
Thou art not *riches*; for that *trash*
Which one age hoards, the next doth wash
And so severely sweep away;
That few remember, where it lay.
So rapid *streams* the wealthy *land*
About them, have at their command:
And shifting *channels* here restore,
There break down, what they banked before.
Thou art not *honour*; for those gay
Feathers will wear, and drop away;
And princes to some upstart *line*
Give new ones, that are full as fine.
Thou art not *pleasure*; for thy *rose*
Upon a *thorn* doth still repose;
Which if not cropped, will quickly shed;
But soon as cropped, grows dull and dead.
    Thou art the *sand*, which fills one *glass*,
And then doth to another pass;
And could I put thee to a stay,
Thou art but *dust*! then go thy way,
And leave me *clean* and bright, though *poor*:
Who stops thee, doth but *daub* his floor,
And *swallow*-like, when he hath done,
To *unknown dwellings* must be gone!
    Welcome pure thoughts and peaceful hours
Enriched with *sunshine* and with *showers*;
Welcome fair hopes and holy cares,
The not to be repented *shares*

Of time and business: the sure *road*
Unto my last and loved *abode*!
                    O supreme *bliss*!
The circle, centre and abyss
Of blessings, never let me miss
Nor leave that *path*, which leads to thee:
Who art alone all things to me!
I hear, I see all the long day
The noise and pomp of the *broad way*;
I note their course and proud approaches:
Their silks, perfumes and glittering coaches.
But in the *narrow way* to thee
I observe only poverty,
And despised things: and all along
The ragged, mean and humble throng
Are still on foot, and as they go,
They sigh and say: *their Lord went so*!
   Give me my *staff* then, as it stood
When green and growing in the wood.
(Those *stones*, which for the *altar* served,
Might not be smoothed, nor finely carved:)
With this *poor stick* I'll pass the *ford*
As *Jacob* did; and thy dear *Word*,
As thou hast dressed it (not as *Wit*
And *depraved tastes* have poisoned it),
Shall in the passage be my meat,
And none else will thy servant eat.
Thus, thus and in no other sort
Will I set forth, though laughed as for't;
And leaving the wise *World* their way,
Go through, though judged to go astray.

Illustrations

Images of Henry Vaughan and his homeland.

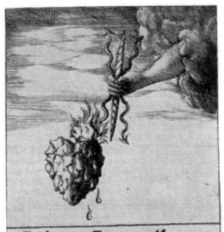

Silex Scintillans:
or
SACRED POEMS
and
Private Eiaculations
By
Henry Vaughan Silurist

LONDON Printed by T.W. for H.Blunden
at ye Castle in Cornehill. 1650

Images of Herefordshire by J.M.W. Turner, this page and over.
River Wye, 1812 (above).

J.M.W. Turner, Tintern Abbey

River Usk (Photo: George Todd)

A Note On John Donne

by A.H. Ninham

John Donne was, Robert Graves said, a 'Muse poet', a poet who wrote passionately of the Muse. It is easy to see Donne as a love poet, in the tradition of love poets such as Bernard de Ventadour, Dante, Petrarch, Cavalcanti, Maurice Scève and Torquato Tasso. Donne has written his fair share of erotic poems. There is the bawdy allusions to the phallus in 'The Flea', while 'The Comparison' parodies the Petrarchan adoration poem, with references to the 'sweat drops of my mistress' breast'. Like Shakespeare in his parody sonnet 'My mistress' eyes are nothing like the sun',[1] Donne sends up the Petrarchan and courtly love genre with gross comparisons ('Like spermatic issue of ripe menstruous boils'). In 'The Bait', there is the archetypal Renaissance opening line 'Come live with me, and be my love', as used by Marlowe and Shakespeare, among others. And there is the complex, ambivalent eroticism of 'The Extasie', a much celebrated poem, and the 19th 'Elegy', where comes his famous

---

1 See Lorna Hutson: "Why the Lady's Eyes Are Nothing Like the Sun", in Isobel Armstrong, ed: *New Feminist Discourses,* Routledge 1992, 154-175; Valerie Wayne, ed: *The Matter of Difference: Materialist Feminist Criticism of Shakespeare*, Harvester Wheatsheaf, 1991

couplet:

> Licence my roving hands, and let them go
> Before, behind, between, above, below.

Helen Gardner writes of 'The Extasie:

> There is no short poem of comparable merit over which such
> completely different views have been expressed, and no lover of Donne's
> poetry can be happy to leave the question in its present state of
> deadlock. For it is obvious that those who assert that the poem is the
> supreme expression of Donne's 'philosophy of love' and those who
> declare that it is a quasi-dramatic piece of special pleading have now no
> hope of converting each other.[2]

Donne's love poems are typical love poems, running through
the gamut of emotions from desire through sex to loathing and
loss and, as ever in Western poetry, death.[3] 'The justification of
natural love as fullness of joy and life is the deepest thought in
Donne's love-poems' writes Herbert Grierson.[4] The *Songs and
Sonnets* celebrate the many faceted emotions of love, emotions
that are so familiar in love poetry from Sappho to Adrienne Rich.
Louis Martz says 'the *Song and sonnets* hold within themselves

2 In "The Argument about *The Ecstasy*", in H. Davis & Helen Gardner, eds:
Elizabethan and Jacobean Studies Presented to F.P. Wilson, Clarendon
Press, Oxford 1959; M.Y. Hughes: "Some of Donne's "Ecstasies"", *Public-
ations of the Modern Language Association of America*, Clarendon Press,
Oxford 1959; M.Y. Hughes: "The Lineage of *The Ecstasy*, *Modern
Language Review*, XXVII, 1932, 1-5.

3 See Claude J. Summers & Ted-Larry Pebworth, eds: *The Eagle and the
Dove: Reassessing John Donne*, University of Missouri Press, Columbia
1986; P. Crutwell: "The Love Poetry of John Donne", in M. Bradbury &
D.Palmer, eds: *Metaphysical Poetry*, Arnold 1970; John A. Clair: "Donne's
'The Canonization"", *Publications of the Modern Language Association
of America*, vol. LXX, 1965, 300-2; J. Bennett: The Love Poetry of John
Donne, in J. Dover Wilson, ed: *Seventeenth Century Studies Presented to
Sir Herbert Grierson*, Clarendon Press, Oxford 1938

4 Quoted in Julian Lovelock, ed, 219

every conceivable attitude toward love threatened by change'.[5] Well, Donne does not quite cover *every* emotion of love, but a good deal of them. In 'The Canonization' we find the age-old Neoplatonic belief that two can become as one ('we two being one', or 'we shall/ Be one', he writes in 'Lovers' Infiniteness'), a common belief in love poetry. In 'The legacy', Donne proposes another common belief – that love for lovers can last an eternity, even though it only lasts an hour or so of external, public, chronological time: 'lovers' hours be full eternity'. In Shakespeare *Sonnets* we find the same concentration on time, on the relation between time and love. Much of Donne's love poetry looks back from the vantage point of old age, as in Thomas Hardy or C.P. Cavafy. 'Love's Alchemy' offers ironic commentaries on the beliefs of the alchemical powers of love which seems to be alchemical glorifying 'elixir', but turns out to be, more often, 'odoriferous':

> So, lovers dream a rich and long delight,
> But get a winter-seeming summer night.

The *Songs and Sonnets* tell the story of love from the viewpoint of a talented, ironic, detached-yet-passionately-involved artist, someone, like Petrarch or Giraut de Borneil, very conscious of how he presents himself in poetry. Always in Donne, as in other love poets, self-consciousness comes to the fore. For in talking of love, Donne is, like Petrarch or Guinicelli, also talking of himself. Indeed, Petrarch's *Rime Sparse* reads as a series of poetic meditations upon the poet's self-in-love: it is the same with John Donne. The *Songs and Sonnets* describe love, yes, but also, rather, how love affects one particular person, how love is experienced by one person, how love is mediated through the rigorous forms of poetry. 'Yet, love and hate me too,' the poet tells his beloved in 'The Prohibition', loving the drama of love, loving to dramatize his love, loving the idea of loving-unto-death,

---

5 Louis Martz: *The Wit of Love*, Notre Dame, 1969

as in the myths of Tristan and Isolde or Anthony and Cleopatra ('Love me, that I may die the gentler way' he implores his lover). Yet in speaking of his beloved, he speaks, really, of himself. Donne's love poetry, like (nearly) all love poetry, is self-reflexive. Although he would 'ne'er parted be', as he writes in 'Song: Sweetest love, I do not go', he knows, too, that love poetry comes out of loss. The beloved woman is not there, so art takes her place. The *Songs and Sonnets* arise from loss, loss of love; they take the place of love. For, if he were clasping his beloved in those feverish embraces as described in 'The Extasie' and 'Elegy', he would not, obviously, bother with poetry. Love poetry has this ambivalent, difficult relationship with love. The poetry is not love, and is no real substitute for it. And writing of love exacerbates the pain and insecurity of the experience of love. The poetry of love becomes vanity (albeit highly sophisticated vanity). Vanity, certainly, is one of the major 'hidden agendas' of the great love poems of the West – Petrarch's *Canzoniere*, Scève's *Délie*, Shakespeare's *Sonnets*, du Bellay's *Sonnets For Helen* and Dante's *Vita Nuova*.

John Donne's poetry is marked by *wit*, by an incisive explorative imagination. Donne is certainly humorous; he parodies existing poetic forms and styles; he is conscious of the foolish positions lovers put themselves in when they concentrate on love to the exclusion of everything else. And Donne produces not a few very memorable poetic moments, not least in that incredible opening to the 'Song', where he writes:

> Go, and catch a falling star,
>   Get with child a mandrake root...

This is a truly wonderful opening of a poem. It must have come to him straight away, out of nowhere, or, rather, straight from the Muse. While 'catching a falling star' may not be too out-of-the-ordinary, 'getting a mandrake root with child' is far more startling. Of course, in the Renaissance era, talk of the magical properties of herbs and plants, talk of witchcraft and healing and the hallucinogenic qualities of *mandragora* was not so unusual as at other times. In our contemporary era, mandrakes are not unknown, for there has been a revival of interest in all things occult, New Age and praeternatural. Even so, Donne's lines are still startling. Those two lines leap at you with total authority, and total quirkiness. The opening establishes itself instantly, and idiosyncratically, like that other quirky line, Before, behind, between, above, below.'

Like Petrarch, Donne is a self-conscious poet who is aware of forming a poetic persona in his poetry. His *Epithalamions*, for instance, are quite different Spenser's marriage songs. Spenser sings breathlessly and lyrically about the promises of love awaiting the couple. Donne is more circumspect, building into his nuptial celebrations hints of disillusion and death. Donne has a piquant death-consciousness, not only apparent in his many *Elegies* for dead people. Spenser too wrote elegies, but Donne's *Elegies* are filled with what we might call a 'modern' awareness of death, with something exhausted, dejected and depressed in it, beyond the usual sorrow and mourning found in, say, Spenser's *Elegies*. Donne's death-consciousness knows the vanity of feeding on 'supernatural food', religion, as he calls it in 'The First Anniversary', *An Anatomy of the World*.

Donne does not keep still: his heightened sense of irony, wit and humour do not allow him to keep still. He cannot be reduced to one viewpoint. Like Shakespeare, Donne is slippery, psychologically, ontologically, metaphysically. The never-ending dialectic of his poetry is expressed in the many contradictions in his lines, as statement is followed by counter-statement, much as in Samuel Beckett. Donne arrives at where he is 'through a series of negatives', to use Lawrence Durrell's phrase. Like Gide, like Petrarch, like the courtly love poets, Donne is not so much in love with love but in love with the poetry of love, with the debate and argument of love. The philosophical slipperiness of Donne's poetry is also expressed in his visual imagery: 'The Extasie', writes Thomas Docherty, one of the best of recent Donne commentators, 'abounds in spatial confusions of the lovers it attempts to describe and circumscribe, with their eye beams crossing, hands cemented, bodies intertwined and so on.' (77) Donne will happily change the gender of the speaker of a poem, or move from a subjective, first person viewpoint to a third person, distanced viewpoint.

A poem that illustrates Donne's brilliant dialectical poesie is found in one of his best poems, 'Upon the Annunciation and Passion Falling Upon One Day, 1608'. Donne is very simple in this poem, which is usually a good start in poetry. Simple and clear. Today, says the narrator, 'My soul eats twice'. He goes on to explore the ambiguities that arise when the moment that the Son of God is conceived in the womb of the Blessed Virgin Mary, on 25 March, Lady Day, the Annunciation, occurs at the same moment that Christ is crucified. Again and again in the poem, Donne investigates how it is that Christ comes into the world and is taken away immediately: 'Christ hither and away...Christ came, and went away'. The simultaneous Annunciation and Passion on 25 March suggests the age-old Western love-death to Donne the Metaphysical poet. For him, the joint Annunciation and Passion of Christianity conjoins the moment of orgasmic joy, the glory of birth, with the moment of intense suffering, the glory of pain. The two moments represent, for Donne, the twin poles of existence: birth and death, or love and death. The Alpha and Omega of life, for Donne, is this love—death duality (or union), like the *yin—yang* dualism in Chinese religion, or the *shiva—shakti* dualism in Hindu religion. Throughout his poetry Donne plays with opposites such as active/ passive, in/ out, hot/ cold, soul/ body, light/ dark, sadness/ ecstasy, sacred/ secular, old/ young, love/ death. These are the basic opposites, or pairs, of poetry. Petrarch employed them profusely, with his 'conceits', those ice/ fire images which were so influential in European poetry. A. E. Dyson and Julian Lovelock speak of 'the extra-

* *252*

ordinary intensity and deviousness of his conceits'.[6] Donne is similarly Petrarchan, and in 'Upon the Annunciation and Passion Falling Upon One Day, 1608', he sees in the fusion of the Annunciation and Passion the ontological poles of life, where 'first and last concur' as he puts it (see page 33). He makes the dichotomies visual, too, he crystallizes the ambiguities with powerful visual images:

Sad and rejoiced she 'seen at once, and
At almost fifty, and at scarce fifteen.

The twin poles of ontology are given different names by Donne, as they are by poets throughout their careers. In Donne sometimes it is being/ non-being, or love/ death, or time/ timelessness. The mystical side of Donne is a powerful undercurrent in his love poetry. In 'The Canonization' he explores the relation of love to time, something that greatly vexed Shakespeare, and which was a major theme of the Sonnets. 'We are tapers too, and at our own cost die' says Donne, hitting the mark in just one line. All we have to do, the narrator tells his beloved, in poem after poem, is *realize*. Realize what exactly? *It.* What? 'we two being one, are it' says Donne. The nowness of life, really, Donne says. The timeless moment, as T. S. Eliot called it in his *Four Quartets*. The moment that is *now*, and *here*. This is ever the aim of mysticism, this ache for the 'two-in-oneness', as Thomas Hardy termed it in *Jude the Obscure*.

There is a good case for seeing Donne as a Muse-orientated poet, a poet who glorifies 'the feminine', in women, and in poetic abstractions. 'O fair love, love's impetuous rage,/ Be my true mistress still' he writes in 'Elegy 16: *On His Mistress.* He adores women, certainly ('what a miracle she was', he writes in 'The Relic'). Donne's relationship to women is ambivalent, as in

---

6 Dyson & Lovelock: "Contracted Thus: 'The Sunne Rising', in Lovelock, ed, 191

Shakespeare or Petrarch.[7] Simultaneously he loves and loathes them. Love and hate exist in a continuum in Donne's mythopoeia of emotion. Studies can be written, and have been written, about Donne's religious sensibilities, about his relation to the Madonna, and to the 'Virgin Queen' of the era, Queen Elizabeth I.[8]

It is easy to rewrite 'John Donne' as a religious poet. By 'rewrite' we mean to 'read' Donne as a religious poet. Indeed, he is often viewed in this way, as one of the 'metaphysical poets' (George Herbert, Richard Crashaw, Henry Vaughan, Thomas Traherne). In the *Holy Sonnets* and *Divine Meditations* Donne comes across as a deeply yearning but also deeply critical religious poet, someone who discourses at length on 'the progress of the soul', while at the same time criticizing both the

7 See, for instance, on Donne, women, eroticism and the Renaissance: Mary Beth Rose, ed: *Women in the Middle Ages and the Renaissance*, Syracuse University Press 1986; Maurer Marget: "The Real Presence of Lucy Russell, Countess of Bedford, and the Terms of John Donne's "Honour is so sublime Perfection", *English Literary History*, XLVII, 1980, 205-35; Ian Maclean: *The Renaissance Notion of Woman*, Cambridge University Press 1985; Stevie Davies: *The idea of Woman in Renaissance literature: The Feminine Reclaimed*, harvester Press, Brighton 1986; Virginia Ramey Molenkott: "John Donne and the limitations of Androgyny", *Journal of English and Germanic Philology*, LXXX, 1981, 22-38; Lindsay Mann: "The typology of Woman in Donne's *Anniversaries*", *Renaissance and Reformation*, 1987, 37-350; David Novarr: *The Disinterred Muse: Donne's Texts and Contexts*, Cornell University Press 1980; Linda Woodbridge: *Women and the English Renaissance: Literature and the Nature of Womankind 1540-1620*, University of Illinois Press, Urbana 1984; R.V. Young: "O my America, my new-found land": Pornography and Imperial Politics in Donne's Elegies", *SC Review*, IV, 1987, 35-48; Lisa Jardine, ed: *Still Harping on Daughters: Women and Drama in the Age of Shakespeare*, Harvester Wheatsheaf 1983; Marianne L. Novy: *Love's Arguments: Gender relations in Shakespeare*, University of North Carolina, Chapel 1984;

8 See Helen Gardner, James Whinny; Julian Lovelock; Carole Levin: "Power, politics, and sexuality: images of Elizabeth I", in Jean R. Brink et al, eds: *The Politics of Gender in Early Modern, Sixteenth Century Studies and Essays*, 12, 1989, 95-110; Leonard Tennenhouse: *Power on Display: The Politics of Shakespeare's Genres*, Methuen 1986; Roy Strong: *The Cult of Elizabeth I*, Thames & Hudson 1977; Peter Stallybrass: "Patriarchal territories", in M. Ferguson et al, eds: *Rewriting the Renaissance*, University of Chicago Press, Chicago 1986, 123-142

'progress' itself and his writing about this 'progress'.[9] This simultaneous exalting and criticizing makes Donne 'modern', though the courtly love poets had cursed themselves for loving, and for writing about love, thus making the pain of love worse. In Donne's religious poems, the usual concerns of traditional Christianity - pain, flesh, lust, death, corruption, punishment, sin, etc - are given a vigorous going over. The *Divine Meditations* abound in extreme emotions - we are constantly reminded of 'joy', 'pain', 'poison', 'doom', 'weeping', 'grief', 'hell', 'sickness' and 'sin'. These are the terms that fill up the *Divine Meditations*. In them religious poems, Donne takes on the great themes of theology and explores with a relentless energy. The two things, though, love and religion, are part of the same experience for Donne, as for so many artists. The passion of love and the passion of God are the sensual and sacred sides of the same phenomena, which is life. The *Songs and Sonnets* are the secular aspect of the existential experience of being alive; the *Holy Sonnets* are the religious dimension. The sacred and profane series of poems pivot around the poet. For what concerns Donne is how love and religion relate to him, to his 'black soul', as he puts it in the fourth of the *Divine Meditations*.

9 See Earl Miner: *The Metaphysical Mode from Donne to Cowley*, Princeton University Press, New jersey 1970; D.L. Peterson: "John Donne's *Holy Sonnets* and the Anglican Doctrine of Contrition", *Studies in Philology*, LVI, 1959, 504-18; F.A. Rowe: *I laugh at Paradise*, Epworth Press 1964; R. Tuve: *Elizabethan and Metaphysical Imagery*, University of Chicago Press 1947; R.L. Colie: "The Rhetoric of Transcendence", *Philological Quarterly*, XLIII, 1964, 145-70; Barbara Kiefer Lewalski: *Protestant Poetics and the Seventeenth Century Religious Lyric*, Princeton University Press, New Jersey, 1979; Dennis Flynn: "Donne's Catholicism: I & II", *Recusant History*, XIII, 1975-6, 1-17, 178-95; Marius Beley: "Religious Cynicism in Donne's Poetry", *Kenyon Review*, XIV, 1952, 619-46

Select Bibliography

N.J.C. Andreasen: *John Donne, Conservative Revolutionary*, Princeton University Press, New Jersey 1967

R.C. Bald: *John Donne: A Life*, Clarendon Press 1970

Ilona Bell: "The Role of the Lady in Donne's *Songs and Sonnets*", *Studies in English Literature*, vol. XXIII, 1983, 113-129

Louis I. Bredvold: *The Religious Thought of Donne in Relation to Medieval and Later Tradition*, Macmillan, New York 1925

John Carey: *John Donne: Life, Mind and Art*, Faber 1981

Charles Monroe Coffin: *John Donne and the New Philosophy*, Columbia University Press, New York 1937

Thomas Docherty: *John Donne, Undone*, Methuen 1986

John Donne: *The Complete English Poems*, ed. A.J. Smith, Penguin 1971

—*Sermons*, eds: G. R. Potter & E.M. Simpson, University of California Press, Berkeley, 1953-62

—*The Elegies and the Songs and Sonnets*, ed Helen Gardner, Clarendon Press 1965

William Empsom: "Donne the space man", *Kenyon Review*, 19, 1957, 337-99

Helen Gardner, ed: *John Donne: A Collection of Critical Essays*, Prentice-Hall, N.J. 1962

Helen Gardner, ed: *John Donne: A Collection of Critical Essays*, Prentice-Hall, New Jersey 1962

Donald L. Guss: *John Donne, Petrarchist*, Wayne State University Press, Detroit 1966;

Marritt Y. Hughes: "Some of Donne's "Ecstasies"", *PMLA*, vol LXXV, 1960, 509-18

Pierre Legouis: *Donne the Craftsman*, Russell & Russell, New York 1962

J.B. Leishman: *The Monarch of Wit*, Hutchinson 1951

Julian Lovelock, ed: *Songs and Sonnets: A Casebook*, Macmillan 1973

Arthur F. Marotti: *John Donne, Coterie Poet*, University of Wisconsin

Press, Madison 1986

Earl Miner: *The Metaphysical Mode from Donne to Cowley*, Princeton University Press, New York 1969

Una Nelly: *The Poet Donne*, Cork University Press, Cork 1969

David Novarr: *The Disinterred Muse Donne's Texts and Contexts*, Cornell University Press 1980

A.C. Partridge: *John Donne: Language and Style*, Andre Deutsch 1978

Maureen Sabine: *Feminine Engendered Faith: The Poetry of John Donne and Richard Crashaw*, Macmillan 1992

Wilbur Sanders: *John Donne's Poetry, Cambridge University Press 1971*

Terry G. Sherwood: *Fulfilling the circle: A Study of John Donne's Thought*, University of Toronto Press 1984

A.J. Smith, ed: *John Donne: The Critical Heritage*, Routledge & Kegan Paul 1975

P.G. Stanwood & Heather Ross Assals, eds: *John Donne and the Theology of Language*, University Press of Columbia 1986

Gary Stringer, ed: *New Essays on Donne*, Universitat Salzburg 1977

James Winny: *A Preface to Donne*, Longman 1970

A Note On Robert Herrick

By M.K. Pace

Robert Herrick (1591-1674) was one of the Cavalier poets (other Cavalier poets included Suckling, Carew and Lovelace). He was born in London and lived much of his life in the rough remoteness of a parish in Devonshire. He studied at Cambridge (St John's College and Trinity Hall), graduating in 1617 as a Bachelor of Arts and a Master of Arts in 1620. His law studies were dropped in 1623, and he was ordained as a deacon and priest in 1624. His major work (*Hesperides or The Works both Humane and Divine* of Robert Herrick Esq.) was published in 1648. There are some 1130 poems in the first, secular part, *Hesperides*, and 272 in *Noble Numbers*, the religious works. F.R. Leavis reckoned that Herrick was 'trivially charming',[1] a view easily refuted by any close perusal of his verse. For T.S. Eliot, Herrick was the paradigmatic 'minor poet'.[2] One can understand how it is that Herrick was for so long viewed in this way. The more one considers his *Hesperides*, though, which one recent critic called 'a seductively sweet, strangely tumultuous exploration of love, art, friendship, festivity, and loss',[3] the greater Robert Herrick becomes.

One of the delights included in this book is Robert Herrick's magnificent 'The Argument of His Book'. This is a truly majestic fourteen-line poem, an invocation to Nature, and of humans interacting with Nature. It is, essentially, a list-poem, where the poet catalogues the things he will sing about in the rest of his book:

> I sing of *Brooks*, of *Blossomes, Birds,* and *Bowers*:
> Of *April, May,* of *June,* and *July*-Flowers.
> I sing of *May-poles, Hock-carts, Wassails, Wakes,*
> Of *Bride-grooms, Brides,* and of their *Bridall-cakes.*
> I write of *Youth,* of *Love,* and have Accesse
> By these, to sing of cleanly-*Wantonesse.*

Herrick couches his list in simple, dramatic English, a form of direct, powerful English that people since Herrick's time have associated with the (King James) Bible. The rest of his poetry (in his *Hesperides*) followed the plan outlined the poem 'The Argument of His Book'. Herrick was particularly well situated, geographically, to write Nature poetry. Like Coleridge, Wordsworth and Brontë, Herrick lived in the midst of the countryside – in the relative isolation of Dean Prior, on the edge of Dartmoor in Devon (he compared his exile with that of Ovid and Horace). Herrick lived in the vicarage in the village halfway between Exeter and Plymouth from 1630 to 1648, and from 1660 to his death, at 83, in 1674. Though at times he fought against the isolation and roughness of his provincial setting,[4] and hankered after the civilization of London, one can see the deep inspiration that the landscape of Devonshire had for Herrick in his poetry. Exiled from the capital and civilized society and culture, Herrick did have his books (his beloved Bible and Latin poets) as well as the friendship of his pets (they appear in his poems, sometimes in heartfelt elegies when they die – such as 'Upon His Spaniel Tracie'), his housekeeper (Prudence Baldwin), his sister, and friends at the nearby Dean Court.

For mediæval, Renaissance and Cavalier poets (like Herrick) Britain would have been a much more 'pastoral' landscape than it is in the 20th century. There would have many more trees, far fewer roads, no cars, planes, trains, electric lights, pylons, pipes, road signs, telephones, and so on. The landscape that poets such as Langland, Chaucer, Wyatt, Parnell, Smith, Keats and Brontë lived in was dramatically different from the urbanized world of the 20th century. There are, of course, continuities between the mediæval and Elizabethan period and now: the same rivers flow, the same birds sing (minus a few species), the same trees rustle their leaves in Autumn. It is (partly) this continuity that makes the poetry of Herrick so enduring. The relationship with Nature is one of those everlasting relationships that humanity is perpetually dealing with (like the relation to the body, to God, to politics). In his poetry Herrick tackles the great themes – love, time, God, Nature, the body.

Much of Herrick's poetry concerns the themes and imagery of Elizabethan (and mediæval) poetry: the evocation of a pastoral, Arcadian, pre-sinful landscape, a Paradise, in fact, populated with shepherdesses, nymphs, animals and the abundance of Nature. Already in Shakespeare this pastoral mythology was fading, being supplanted by a worldly knowingness (if not cynicism). Herrick's poetry, though, often harks back to a paradisal earlier age, and rues the passing of time that has changed it all (for the worse, in his opinion). We find the same Greek, Roman, Biblical, mediæval, Christian and Renaissance/ humanist themes in Herrick's work that are the staple of Elizabethan poetry.[5] As well as learned and literary, Herrick's subjects are often seemingly 'ordinary' or 'common-place'. He writes of bucolic traditions; of old age; of bawdy times; of his mistress's breasts; of cherry blossom; of fashionable clothes (one of his famous poems is 'Delight in Disorder', where 'a careless shoestring' betokens a 'wild civility' which 'bewitches' the poet more than precision).

There are many poems in Herrick's work of love – about love desired, lost and mourned. Herrick is very definitely a 'Muse poet', to use Robert Graves's term. There are many poems to various mistresses, 'my dearest Beauties' he calls them in 'To His

Lovely Mistresses' (Anthea, Perilla, Electra, Blanch, Judith, Silvia, and the most beloved of all, Julia). There are many poems to certain 'muses' or 'maidens'. The sheer number (and quality) of Herrick's poems to Julia attests to his deep passion for women, the friendship and strength of women: 'To Julia', 'To Roses in Julia's Bosom', 'To the Fever Not to Trouble Julia', 'Julia's Petticoat', 'The Frozen Zone: or, Julia Disdainful', 'To Julia, in Her Dawn, or Daybreak', 'His Last Request to Julia', 'The Parliament of Roses to Julia', 'Upon Julia's Recovery', 'Upon Julia's Fall', 'His Sailing From Julia', 'His Embalming to Julia', 'Her Legs', 'Her Bed', 'On Julia's Picture', 'The Bracelet to Julia', 'A Ring Presented to Julia', 'To Julia in the Temple' and so on. Apart from poems addressed 'To His Book', there are probably more poems in Herrick's work 'To Julia' than to anything else. Julia is 'the prime of *Paradise*' ('To Julia, in Her Dawn, or Daybreake'). She is utterly adored, often erotically. There are many poems which eulogize her breasts and nipples, for instance: 'Display thy breasts.../ Between whose glories, there my lips I'll lay,/ Ravisht' he writes (in 'Upon Julia's Breasts'); other pæans to Julia's breasts include 'Upon the Roses in Julia's Bosom' and 'Upon the Nipples of Julia's Breast'. Herrick makes the age-old connections between the fertility of Nature outside (the rain, the lush vegetation, the rivers of the Paradisal Earth) and the bounty of women inside (Julia's breasts form a valley of abundance, as in Shakespeare's 'Venus and Adonis', in which the poet would like to languish). Women in Herrick's poetry are seen as the givers of pleasure (expressed as sex), nurturance (breast milk), and all things worthy in the world (love). 'All Pleasures meet in Womankind' he writes in 'On Himself'. They are just as important in his poetry as God, the King or Christianity. Much of Herrick's poetry concerns (masculine) public, worldly, and religious themes (such as King Charles and politics, or God and the Bible), but just as much (more, probably) celebrates (feminine) erotic pleasure, food, Nature, folk rituals, music and women, in that 'cleanly-wanton' way which is Herrick's own (the phrase, which describes much of his work, comes from the opening poem of *Hesperides*).

Herrick happily fuses erotic descriptions of Nature or food with lush, sensual evocations of erotic love.6 To describe how wonderful sensual love can be, Herrick, like so many poets before him, uses the metaphor of abundant Nature, expressed in flowers, trees, rivers, hills, and food. In 'To Phillis To love, and Love With Him', for example, Herrick's narrator proclaims:

Live, live with me, and thou shalt see
The pleasures I'll prepare for thee...

And goes into a long list of the bounty of Nature: 'sweet soft Moss shall by thy bed', 'Fleeces purest Downe', 'Cream of Cowslips buttered', daisies, violets, daffodils, primroses, roses, the 'blushing Apple, bashful Peare,/ And shame-fac't Plum'. Herrick's poetry is, like Shelley's or Shakespeare's, tremendously sensual. In poem after poem he uses metaphors and images of shiny, ripe fruit, or radiant flowers, or soft grass, or silk, or fresh springwater. Images of natural abundance occur throughout his poetry. Even rain, which he would have known day after day in Dartmoor, is treated spectrally, as in 'A Conjuration to Electra', where he speaks of the 'Dewes and drisling Raine,/ That swell the Golden Graine'. Some of the most erotic poems around concerning perfume and smell are Herrick's: In 'Love Perfumes All Parts' Herrick writes of his mistress Anthea's body in a state of heightened intoxication, claiming that her hands, thighs and legs 'are all/ Richly Aromatical'. So deliciously musky is the beloved for the poet, he says she is sweeter than Juno and muskier than the Goddess Isis, no less.

Some of Herrick's best landscape poems are not about Dartmoor or Devonshire, but about London, his birthplace and beloved city. 'His Return to London' is perhaps the best of these city-poems, in which his return to the capital is seen as a yearned-for homecoming.

O *Place! O People!* Manners! fram'd to please
All *Nations, Customers, Kindreds, Language!*

There are poems in Herrick's *œuvre* on the pleasures of music, which he calls 'thou *Queen of Heaven,* Care-charming-spel' (in 'To Musick. A Song'). The theme of the music-poems is the enchantment that music can bring. 'Charm me asleep, and melt me so/ With thy Delicious Numbers' he urges music in 'To Musique, To Becalme His Fever'. 'And make me smooth as Balme, and Oile againe' he entreats in 'To Musick'.

There are some hearty and tender pæans to holidays, feasts, festivals and rituals (pagan as well as Christian) in Herrick's poetry: such as 'The Succession of Four Sweet Months', and the best of them all, Corinna's Going a Maying'. The celebration of the seasons and annual holidays chimes with Herrick's abiding theme of the passing of time, and the need to seize the moment and enjoy it.

Some of Herrick's most delightful poems are about the wonders of Nature, such as blossoms, flowers and fields ('The Shower of Blossoms', 'The Lilly in a Christal', 'To Pansies', 'To Cherry-blossomes', 'To a Bed of Tulips', 'To Laurels', 'Upon Roses, 'The Succession of Four Sweet Months', 'The Rainbow', 'To the Rose: Song', 'To Flowers', 'To Blossoms', 'To Groves', 'To Violets', 'To Carnations', 'To Sycamores', 'To Springs and Fountains', 'To Daffadills', 'To Meddowes', 'To the Willow-tree' and 'To Prim-roses Fill'd With Morning-dew').

It's typical of Herrick, too, to mention in his Nature poems the passing of time. The very first verse of his 'To Blossoms' asks the question of the blossoms 'Why do ye fall so fast?' As soon as the beauty of the blossoms is invoked, time and death follow on immediately. The line of 'To Blossoms' is 'They glide/ Into the grave.' The same protestations to Nature's pleasures being over so swiftly occur in 'To Daisies, Not To Shut So Soone' and 'To Daffadills' ('we weep to see/ You haste away so soone'). In 'All Things Decay and Die' he states quite baldly: *'All things decay with Time'.*

The many poems 'To His Book' attest to Herrick's deep concern for his art - how long (or if) it will last, who will enshrine it, and soon. The same concerns with the relations between mortality, time and death and the artist and his art are central to Shakespeare's *œuvre* (it is the guiding theme of the *Sonnets*). The key Herrick theme is to enjoy life before death takes it away. 'While Fate permits us, let's be merry' as he puts it in 'To Enjoy the Time'. 'Every time seems so short to be' he says in 'Felicity, Quick of Flight'.

It's true that Robert Herrick did not write long poems, like Shelley or Wordsworth (in the sense that long, 'epic' poems equal seriousness and *gravitas*),[7] but, in his own way, his Nature poetry is every bit as valuable as theirs. His love-poetry is sometimes compared unfavourably with that of John Donne: again, in his own way, Herrick is every bit as fruitful a love-poet as Donne (or Campion, Marlowe, even Shakespeare or Spenser). He was not as showy a poet as Coleridge or Pope, not so ambitious, formally, yet he is a superb writer, witty, hedonistic, impassioned, commonsensical.

•

I have modernized some of the spellings in Herrick's poems, but have kept his capitalizations and use of italics. These are part of the flavour of Herrick's verse, and do not detract, I think, from the power or nuance of his poetry. I have chosen more of his poems from the secular book *Hesperides* than from the religious volume *Noble Numbers*, not only because there are simply many more poems in *Hesperides*, but also because *Hesperides* contains his best work.

Notes

1. F.R. Leavis: *Revaluation*, Chatto & Windus 1936, 36
2. T.S. Eliot: "What is Minor Poetry?", *Swanee Review*, 54, 1946
3. Leah S. Marcus: "Robert Herrick", in Coms, 1993, 180
4. In 'Discontents in Devon' Herrick writes:

More discontents I never had
Since I was born, then here;
Where I have been, and still am sad,
In this dull *Devon-shire*...

5. In his poetry Herrick alludes to, among others, Anacreon, Horace, Catullus, Marital and other (Roman) poets, as well as Ben Jonson (whom Herrick admired) and the *Bible*.

6. As Stephen Coote puts it, in Herrick's poetry the 'sensuousness is the more telling for its sophisticated simplicity and, at its best, is returned to nature.' (Coote: *The Penguin Short History of English Literature*, Penguin 1993, 175)

7. There are lengthy poems (such as 'Upon His Kinswoman Mistress Elizabeth Herrick', 'His Age, Dedicated To His Peculiar Friend, M. John Wickes, Under the Name of Posthumus', 'A Nuptial Song, or Epithalamie, on Sir Clipseby Crew and His Lady', 'Corinna's Going a Maying', 'A Country Life: To His Brother, M. Tho: Herrick', 'The Welcome to Sack' and 'An Epithalamie to Sir Thomas Southwell and His Ladie') but nothing as long as *Prometheus Unbound* or *The Prelude*.

Bibliography

Cleanth Brooks: *The Well Wrought Urn*, Dennis Dobson 1957

A.B. Coiro: *Robert Herrick's 'Hesperides' and the Epigram Book Tradition*, John Hopkins University Press 1988

—ed: *Robert Herrick*, special no. of *George Herbert Journal* 14, 1-2, Autumn 1990

N. Coms, ed: *The Cambridge Companion to English Poetry: Donne to Marvell*, Cambridge University Press 1993

R.H. Deming: *Ceremony and Art: Robert Herrick's Poetry*, Mouton, Hague 1974

A. Leigh Deneef: *'This Poetick Liturgie': Robert Herrick's Ceremonial Mode*, Duke University Press 1974

E.H. Hageman: *Robert Herrick: A Reference Guide*, G.K. Hall, Boston 1983

G. Hammond: *Fleeting Things: English Poets and Poems 1616-1660*, Harvard University Press 1990

Robert Herrick: *The Poems of Robert Herrick*, ed. L.C. Martin, Oxford University Press 1965

—*Poems*, ed. J. Max Patrick, New York University Press 1963

—*Robert Herrick: The Hesperides and Noble Numbers*, ed. Alfred Pollard, Muse's Library, London 1891

—*The Poetical Works of Robert Herrick,* Oxford English Texts 1915

—*Hesperides: The Poems and Other Remains of Robert Herrick Now First Collected*, ed. W. Carew Hazlitt, London 1869

—*The Complete Works of Robert Herrick*, ed. Alexander B. Grosart, London 1876

—*Selected Poems*, ed. David Jesson-Dibley, Carcanet 1989

M. MacLeod: *Concordance to the Poems of Robert Herrick*, Oxford University Press, New York 1936

Leah S. Marcus: *The Politics of Mirth: Jonson, Herrick, Milton, Marvell and the Defense of Old Holiday Pastimes*, University of Chicago Press 1986

F.W. Moorman: *Robert Herrick: a Biographical and Critical Study*,

Russell & Russell, New York 1910

S. Musgrove: "The Universe of Robert Herrick", *Auckland University College Bulletin*, 38, 1950

John Press: *Herrick*, Longmans, Green & Co

Roger Rollin: *Robert Herrick*, Twayne, New York 1966/92

—& J. Max Patrick, eds: *Trust to Good Verses: Herrick Tercentenary Essays*, University of Pittsburgh Press 1977

George W. Scott: *Robert Herrick,* Sidgwick & Jackson 1974

A Note On Henry Vaughan

By A.H. Ninham

Henry Vaughan is the Metaphysical poet[10] from the Welsh borders (he was born at Newton-upon-Usk, Breconshire, in 1621). He went up to Oxford in 1638, studied law in London, returned to live in Breconshire around 1642, wrote some astonishing religious poetry, and died in 1695 in Scethrog. He married twice (in 1646 and 1655), and had eight children.

Henry Vaughan's poetry is marked by a 'deep, but dazzling darkness', as the poet writes in one of his most famous poems, 'The Night'. This dazzling night pervades Henry Vaughan's poetry. It is a cosmic night, a night of regeneration. Many of the Vaughan's poems collected here pivot around an experience of the cosmic, religious night, from 'The World', with its famous, much-anthologized opening lines:

I saw Eternity the other night
Like a great *Ring* of pure and endless light.

---

10 The other Metaphysical poets included Robert Herrick, George Herbert, Richard Crashaw, Andrew Marvell and John Donne.

It is a night of rebirth, the night as a dark womb, in which the world is reborn. Cosmic rebirth is one of the major themes in Vaughan's poetry, and especially in his series of sacred poems, *Silex Scintillans* (1650; enlarged 1655). 'Regeneration, the initial and dominant concern of *Silex Scintillans*, is a natural process: spiritual regeneration is approached and comprehended by drawing upon other and more immediately accessible modes of experience', writes Thomas O. Calhoun (p.128).

Henry Vaughan's poetry is about big themes, cosmic themes, religious themes, with titles such as 'The World', 'Regeneration', 'Peace', and 'The Retreat'. Vaughan is not shy of big themes, as some poets are. He dives right in. His openings are particular powerful, striking up a majestic tone immediately:

I saw Eternity the other night
Like a great *Ring* of pure and endless light... ('The World')

Happy those early days! when I
Shined in my Angel-infancy. ('The Retreat')

'My soul, there is a country
　　　Far beyond the stars... ('Peace')

They are all gone into the world of light!
　　　And I alone sit ling'ring here... ("They are all gone")

Through that pure *Virgin-shine*,
That sacred veil drawn o'er the glorious noon... ('The Night')

Stately lines these, which announce instantly the high-minded, serious, religious nature of the poems. Henry Vaughan tackles, like the other Metaphysical poets, the grand themes of life: birth, death, love, God, faith, doubt, nature and the self. His goal is rebirth, transformation, metamorphosis, call it what you will. Always there is movement in Vaughan's verse. As Helen O'Grady writes:

At the level of sensory thought, Vaughan's emphasis is always on activity, the dynamic quality of impressions. His vital world is constantly moving,

✳ 270

changing, a kaleidoscope of light and shadow and dynamic forms.[11]

It is a religious journey that Henry Vaughan takes us on, from confusion and insecurity through a night of shadows, a 'Dark Night of the Soul', to use St John of the Cross's term, to a final winning-through to harmony, even unity. Not all of Vaughan's lyrics are religious in nature; indeed, we have included some of his 'secular' poems here, which deal in the more traditional, familiar manner with love. His religious poems, though, are his finest achievement, where he charts the 'progress of the soul'.

Henry Vaughan's poetry builds on a foundation of mysticism, the mysticism of Meister Eckhart, who spoke of going 'from nothingness to nothingness', St John of the Cross, and visionaries such as Dionysius and Hildegard of Bingen. Whether Henry Vaughan knew of these mystics or not is not our concern here: his poetry comes from that form of ecstatic, Christian mysticism.

Henry Vaughan is one of the most radiant of British poets. Like other Metaphysical poets (poets such as George Herbert, Richard Crashaw, Andrew Marvell and John Donne), the deep, dazzling darkness of the alchemical ferment in Vaughan's poetry is balanced by a radiance, a light shining out of the darkness. This is a divine light, as found in the *Mystical Theology* of the very influential writer, Dionysius the Areopagite (*c.* 500). Dionysius' Neoplatonic visions of divinity and the celestial hierarchies of angels influenced Dante Alighieri, among many other poets. In Dionysius, light and dark are used as elementary, primæval manifestations of religious, cosmic forces, as in Gnosticism and Zorasterianism. It is not simply a case of God versus Satan, or good versus evil. That dualism is important in Neoplatonic and Christian philosophy, but it is not the whole picture. Instead, there is an emphasis on harmony, on the synthesis of opposites, which is a primary function of mythology and religion. Taoism has its *yin* and *yang* elements, where the dark contains the seed of the light, and vice versa. Each flows into the next. It is the

11 Quoted in A. Rudrun: *Henry Vaughan*, 62.

same with Metaphysical poetry, and with Henry Vaughan. His poetry moves from dark to light, with the seeds of one being always present in the other. His nights, for all their darkness, also grow light.

Henry Vaughan's Metaphysical philosophy is a combination of Christian and Neoplatonic thought. Vaughan's Neoplatonism include a variety of hermetic approaches. Most prominent, perhaps, is alchemy and pursuits associated with it – Rosicrucianism, for instance, and Western magic. Critics have written illuminatingly on the elements of magic and Neoplatonism in William Shakespeare's plays, the Elizabethans and the Metaphysical poets.[12] Henry and his brother Thomas were interested in various components of hermetic philosophy, including the great alchemist Paracelsus, the collection of writings called 'Hermes Trismegistus', Cornelius Agrippa's *De Occulta Philosophia*, the alchemical treatise *Theatricum Chemicum*, and the *Oracles* of Zoroaster.[13]

There is not space here to deal in depth with the hermetic/ Neoplatonic/ alchemical elements in Henry Vaughan's poetry. Usually the Metaphysical poets are viewed in relation solely to Christian thinking. But the more one finds out about them, the more their philosophy tends towards the alternatives to Christianity – alchemy, Neoplatonism, magic, numerology, Rosicrucianism, Qabbalism, and so on. Indeed, these philosophies all operate within the Judæo-Christian tradition, and poets do not see any conflict, necessarily, between the 'One and All' of Neo-

---

12 See, for example: Ted Hughes: *Shakespeare and the Goddess of Complete Being*, Faber, 1992; Frances Yates: *The Rosicrucian Enlightenment*, Routledge, 1972 and *Giordano Bruno and the Hermetic Tradition*, Vintage Books, New York, 1969; D.P. Walker: *Spiritual and Demonic Magic from Ficino to Campanella*, Warburg Institute, 1958; Wayne Shumaker: *The Occult Sciences in the Renaissance*, University of California Press, Berkeley, Calif., 1972; Walter Pagel: *Paracelsus: An Introduction to Philosophical Medicine in the Era of the Renaissance*, Karger, New York, 1958; Peter French: *John Dee*, Routledge, 1972.

13 See A. Rudrun: *Henry Vaughan*, 4; T. Calhoun, 53f; E. Martin; R.Durr.

platonism and the God of Judæo-Christianity. Renaissance philosophy brought together Christianity and pantheism, Christianity and Neoplatonism. Poets see unity, and multiplicity in unity. For them, there is not necessarily a conflict between nature worship and God worship. For Vaughan, pantheistic, nature mysticism is not at odds with monotheic Christianity. All things, rather, are united – in Vaughan's case by the visionary experience of the poet.

In Henry Vaughan's work, we are always aware of the sky, the vast, wheeling sky, as with the poesie of William Shakespeare and Rainer Maria Rilke. Vaughan's sky is, of course, filled with celestial music, the 'music of the universe' as Boethius called it.[14] There is music in nature, a harmony. There is a song in the heart of the world, poets believe, and Vaughan sings it. 'Song is existence', as Rilke wrote in his *Sonnets to Orpheus*. Many poets have sung the song of nature, much as the ancestor-gods of the Australian aborigines 'sung' the world into existence. At this primal level, at the level of Creation mythologies, poetry and music fuse, forming a continuum embodied in one figure, the shaman.

The world's mysteries can be 'sung' by the poet. 'The poet, like the alchemist, can make nature "speak"', writes Thomas Calhoun in his study of Henry Vaughan (106). The poet discovers them, or simply uncovers them so that people can experience them. They were *always* there. Life is always rich, even blissful. One simply has to be aware of it. Poets such as Vaughan, Rainer Maria Rilke, Johann Wolfgang von Goethe, Arthur Rimbaud and Edmund Spenser try to make these mysteries or 'streams' of life, as the poet Peter Redgrove calls them,[15] clear to all. These sound like very high-flown claims, yet Henry Vaughan is always a poet who

14 Boethius: *De institutione musica*, 1.3, in Gottfried Friedlin: *Source Readings in Music History*, ed. Oliver Strunk, Norton, New York, 1950, 86.

15 See Peter Redgrove: *The Black Goddess and the Sixth Sense*, Bloomsbury, 1987

deals, like Richard Crashaw or Thomas Hardy, in 'serious' themes.

It's romantic, perhaps, to think that Henry Vaughan's nature mysticism was inspired partly by his surroundings, the hills and vales of Wales, which are very beautiful. Alan Rudrun writes:

> This quality in Vaughan's poetry is related, one feels sure, to the fact of his living in the Usk Valley, with its shifting sunshine, cloud and shower and the incessant sound of running water...[16]

When we look at Henry Vaughan's poetry, we see an immense love of nature and natural forms. Not just skies, but flowers, mountains, rivers, and so on. Vaughan's nature poetry, though, is overlaid or, rather, powered by a radiant language. So rivers are not mere channels of water, but shining ribbons winding through the world. Clouds are not simply clouds, they are golden clouds. Vaughan's nature poetry becomes, all the time, symbolic. His poems feature protagonists who are on pilgrimages, who travel through a world lit by 'pure Virgin-shine'. The 'Virgin-shine' is a good term, laden with mystery, to define the light that suffuses Vaughan's poetry. His poems are descriptions of what the poet sees during his voyages through the 'Virgin-shine' world.

Look at 'Looking Back': it is typical of Henry Vaughan's work, featuring a pilgrimage through a religious landscape, a landscape at once natural and magical. Vaughan throws a religious radiance around landscapes, so they glow. So in 'To His Books', he opens with 'Bright books!', and in 'Midnight' he describes heaven as a 'fiery-liquid light'. Everywhere there is radiance in Vaughan's poetry, but this radiance has to gained and won, after the struggle through the Dark Night of the Soul. The ecstasy, when it comes, is intense, as ecstasies tend to be. 'The Morning-Watch' is a poem of 'coming through', as D.H. Lawrence put it. It is a poem of extreme joy, like Arthur Rimbaud's 'Morning of Ecstasy' from his *Illuminations*. Metaphysical poetry is full of extreme statements,

---

16 A. Rudrun: *Henry Vaughan*, 63

often of religious rapture, and often accompanied by exclamation marks. True, Percy Bysshe Shelley and John Keats use more exclamation marks than Henry Vaughan or John Donne, but in 'The Morning-Watch', Vaughan celebrates his rebirth in grand style:

> O joys! infinite sweetness! with what flowers,
> And shoots of glory, my soul breaks, and buds!
> > All the long hours
> > Of night, and rest
> > Through the still shrouds
> > Of sleep, and clouds,
> This dew fell on my breast...

Henry Vaughan's poetry is optimistic, at times idealistic, if being alive to life is being idealistic. His poetry is, ultimately, a poetry of celebration, whereas some other poets end up reflecting negatively on life, without offering any remedies. Vaughan of course is a believer, and his faith in God buoys him up in his darkest moments. He does not dredge the depths of despair, as some mystics have done. He sees God in nature and celebrates this vision.

Bibliography

Don Cameron Allen: "Henry Vaughan's 'Salome on Ice'", *Philological Quarterly*, 23, 1944, 84-5

—. "Henry Vaughan: "Cock Crowing", *Image and Meaning: Metaphoric Traditions in Renaissance Poetry*, John Hopkins University Press, Baltimore, 1960

Edmund Blunden: *On the Poems of Henry Vaughan: Characteristics and Intimations*, Richard Cobden-Sanderson, 1927

Robert E. Bourdette: "Recent Studies in Henry Vaughan", *English Literary Renaissance*, IV no.2, 1974, 299-310

Thomas O. Calhoun: *Henry Vaughan: The Achievement of* Silex Scintillans, University of Delaware Press/ Associated University Press, New Jersey, 1981

A.U. Chapman: "Henry Vaughan and magnetic philosophy", *Southern Review* (Adelaide), IV, iii, 1971, 215-26

R.A. Durr: *On the Mystical Poetry of Henry Vaughan*, Harvard University Press, Cambridge, Mass., 1962

Kenneth Friedenreich: *Henry Vaughan*, Twayne Publishers, Boston, 1978

Ross Garner: *Henry Vaughan: Experience and Tradition*, University of Chicago Press, Chicago, 1959

Elizabeth Holmes: *Henry Vaughan and the Hermetic Philosophy*, Blackwell, 1932

Merritt Y. Hughes: "The theme of pre-existence and infancy in 'The Retreat'", *Philogical Quarterly*, XX, 1941, 484-500

F.E. Hutchinson: *Henry Vaughan: A Life and Interpretation*, Clarendon Press, 1971

A.CC. Judson: "The Source of Henry Vaughan's Ideas Concerning God in Nature", *Studies in Philology*, XXIV, 1927, 592-606

Frank Kermode: "The Private Imagery of Henry Vaughan", *Review of English Studies*, N.S., 1, 1950

E.L. Martin: "Henry Vaughan and 'Hermes Tristmegistus'", *Review of English Studies*, 18, July, 1942, 302-4

—. "Henry and Thomas Vaughan", *Modern Language Review*, 39, 1944, 180-3

W.R. Parker: "Henry Vaughan and his Publishers", *The Library*, 4th series, 20, 1940, 40, 1-6

Jonathan F.S. Post: "Vaughan's 'The Night' and his 'late and dusky' Age", *Studies in English Literature*, 19, 1970, 127-141

Mary Eileen Rickey: "Vaughan, *The Temple*, and Poetic Form", *Studies in Philology*, 59, 1962, 162-170

Alan Rudrun: *Henry Vaughan,* University of Wales Press, 1981

—. "The Influence of Alchemy in the Poems of Henry Vaughan", *Philological Quarterly*, 49, 1970, 469-80

—. "Henry Vaughan's 'The Book': a hermetic poem', *Journal of the Australian Universities Language and Literature Association*, 1961, 161-6

—. "Henry Vaughan and the theme of transfiguration", *Southern Review*, I, 1963, 54-68

—. "Vaughan's 'The Night': some hermetic notes', *Modern Language Review*, LXIV, 1969, 11-19

J.D. Simmonds: *Masques of God: Form and Theme in the Poetry of Henry Vaughan*, University of Pittsburgh Press, Pittsburgh, 1972

A.J. Smith: "Henry Vaughan's Ceremony of Innocence", *Essays and Studies*, N.S., 26, 1973, 35-52

E.M. Williamson: *Henry Vaughan*, Welsh Home Service, 1953

WEBSITE

luminarium.org

CRESCENT MOON PUBLISHING

web: www.crmoon.com e-mail: cresmopub@yahoo.co.uk

ARTS, PAINTING, SCULPTURE

The Art of Andy Goldsworthy
Andy Goldsworthy: Touching Nature
Andy Goldsworthy in Close-Up
Andy Goldsworthy: Pocket Guide
Andy Goldsworthy In America

Land Art: A Complete Guide
The Art of Richard Long
Richard Long: Pocket Guide
Land Art In the UK
Land Art in Close-Up
Land Art In the U.S.A.
Land Art: Pocket Guide
Installation Art in Close-Up
Minimal Art and Artists In the 1960s and After
Colourfield Painting
Land Art DVD, TV documentary
Andy Goldsworthy DVD, TV documentary
The Erotic Object: Sexuality in Sculpture From Prehistory to the Present Day
Sex in Art: Pornography and Pleasure in Painting and Sculpture
Postwar Art
Sacred Gardens: The Garden in Myth, Religion and Art
Glorification: Religious Abstraction in Renaissance and 20th Century Art
Early Netherlandish Painting

Leonardo da Vinci
Piero della Francesca
Giovanni Bellini
Fra Angelico: Art and Religion in the Renaissance
Mark Rothko: The Art of Transcendence

Frank Stella: American Abstract Artist
Jasper Johns
Brice Marden
Alison Wilding: The Embrace of Sculpture
Vincent van Gogh: Visionary Landscapes

Eric Gill: Nuptials of God
Constantin Brancusi: Sculpting the Essence of Things
Max Beckmann
Caravaggio
Gustave Moreau

Egon Schiele: Sex and Death In Purple Stockings
Delizioso Fotografico Fervore: Works In Process 1
Sacro Cuore: Works In Process 2
The Light Eternal: J.M.W. Turner
The Madonna Glorified: Karen Arthurs

LITERATURE

J.R.R. Tolkien: The Books, The Films, The Whole Cultural Phenomenon
J.R.R. Tolkien: Pocket Guide
Tolkien's Heroic Quest
The *Earthsea* Books of Ursula Le Guin
Beauties, Beasts and Enchantment: Classic French Fairy Tales
German Popular Stories by the Brothers Grimm
Philip Pullman and *His Dark Materials*
Sexing Hardy: Thomas Hardy and Feminism
Thomas Hardy's *Tess of the d'Urbervilles*
Thomas Hardy's *Jude the Obscure*
Thomas Hardy: The Tragic Novels
Love and Tragedy: Thomas Hardy
The Poetry of Landscape in Hardy
Wessex Revisited: Thomas Hardy and John Cowper Powys
Wolfgang Iser: Essays and Interviews
Petrarch, Dante and the Troubadours
Maurice Sendak and the Art of Children's Book Illustration
Andrea Dworkin
Cixous, Irigaray, Kristeva: The *Jouissance* of French Feminism
Julia Kristeva: Art, Love, Melancholy, Philosophy, Semiotics and Psychoanalysis
Hélene Cixous I Love You: The *Jouissance* of Writing
Luce Irigaray: Lips, Kissing, and the Politics of Sexual Difference
Peter Redgrove: Here Comes the Flood
Peter Redgrove: Sex-Magic-Poetry-Cornwall
Lawrence Durrell: Between Love and Death, East and West
Love, Culture & Poetry: Lawrence Durrell
Cavafy: Anatomy of a Soul
German Romantic Poetry: Goethe, Novalis, Heine, Hölderlin
Feminism and Shakespeare
Shakespeare: Love, Poetry & Magic
The Passion of D.H. Lawrence
D.H. Lawrence: Symbolic Landscapes
D.H. Lawrence: Infinite Sensual Violence
Rimbaud: Arthur Rimbaud and the Magic of Poetry
The Ecstasies of John Cowper Powys
Sensualism and Mythology: The Wessex Novels of John Cowper Powys
Amorous Life: John Cowper Powys and the Manifestation of Affectivity (H.W. Fawkner)
Postmodern Powys: New Essays on John Cowper Powys (Joe Boulter)
Rethinking Powys: Critical Essays on John Cowper Powys
Paul Bowles & Bernardo Bertolucci
Rainer Maria Rilke
Joseph Conrad: *Heart of Darkness*
In the Dim Void: Samuel Beckett
Samuel Beckett Goes into the Silence
André Gide: Fiction and Fervour
Jackie Collins and the Blockbuster Novel
Blinded By Her Light: The Love-Poetry of Robert Graves
The Passion of Colours: Travels In Mediterranean Lands
Poetic Forms

POETRY

Ursula Le Guin: Walking In Cornwall
Peter Redgrove: Here Comes The Flood
Peter Redgrove: Sex-Magic-Poetry-Cornwall
Dante: Selections From the Vita Nuova
Petrarch, Dante and the Troubadours
William Shakespeare: Sonnets
William Shakespeare: Complete Poems
Blinded By Her Light: The Love-Poetry of Robert Graves
Emily Dickinson: Selected Poems
Emily Brontë: Poems
Thomas Hardy: Selected Poems
Percy Bysshe Shelley: Poems
John Keats: Selected Poems
Joh n Keats: Poems of 1820
D.H. Lawrence: Selected Poems
Edmund Spenser: Poems
Edmund Spenser: Amoretti
John Donne: Poems
Henry Vaughan: Poems
Sir Thomas Wyatt: Poems
Robert Herrick: Selected Poems
Rilke: Space, Essence and Angels in the Poetry of Rainer Maria Rilke
Rainer Maria Rilke: Selected Poems
Friedrich Hölderlin: Selected Poems
Arseny Tarkovsky: Selected Poems
Arthur Rimbaud: Selected Poems
Arthur Rimbaud: A Season in Hell
Arthur Rimbaud and the Magic of Poetry
Novalis: Hymns To the Night
German Romantic Poetry
Paul Verlaine: Selected Poems
Elizaethan Sonnet Cycles
D.J. Enright: By-Blows
Jeremy Reed: Brigitte's Blue Heart
Jeremy Reed: Claudia Schiffer's Red Shoes
Gorgeous Little Orpheus
Radiance: New Poems
Crescent Moon Book of Nature Poetry
Crescent Moon Book of Love Poetry
Crescent Moon Book of Mystical Poetry
Crescent Moon Book of Elizabethan Love Poetry
Crescent Moon Book of Metaphysical Poetry
Crescent Moon Book of Romantic Poetry
Pagan America: New American Poetry

MEDIA, CINEMA, FEMINISM and CULTURAL STUDIES

J.R.R. Tolkien: The Books, The Films, The Whole Cultural Phenomenon
J.R.R. Tolkien: Pocket Guide
The *Lord of the Rings* Movies: Pocket Guide
The Cinema of Hayao Miyazaki
Hayao Miyazaki: *Princess Mononoke*: Pocket Movie Guide
Hayao Miyazaki: *Spirited Away*: Pocket Movie Guide
Tim Burton : Hallowe'en For Hollywood
Ken Russell
Ken Russell: *Tommy*: Pocket Movie Guide
The Ghost Dance: The Origins of Religion
The Peyote Cult

Cixous, Irigaray, Kristeva: The *Jouissance* of French Feminism
Julia Kristeva: Art, Love, Melancholy, Philosophy, Semiotics and Psychoanalysis
Luce Irigaray: Lips, Kissing, and the Politics of Sexual Difference
Hélene Cixous I Love You: The *Jouissance* of Writing
Andrea Dworkin
'Cosmo Woman': The World of Women's Magazines
Women in Pop Music
HomeGround: The Kate Bush Anthology
Discovering the Goddess (Geoffrey Ashe)
The Poetry of Cinema
The Sacred Cinema of Andrei Tarkovsky
Andrei Tarkovsky: Pocket Guide
Andrei Tarkovsky: *Mirror*: Pocket Movie Guide
Andrei Tarkovsky: *The Sacrifice*: Pocket Movie Guide
Walerian Borowczyk: Cinema of Erotic Dreams
Jean-Luc Godard: The Passion of Cinema
Jean-Luc Godard: *Hail Mary*: Pocket Movie Guide
Jean-Luc Godard: *Contempt*: Pocket Movie Guide
Jean-Luc Godard: *Pierrot le Fou*: Pocket Movie Guide
John Hughes and Eighties Cinema
Ferris Bueller's Day Off: Pocket Movie Guide
Jean-Luc Godard: Pocket Guide
The Cinema of Richard Linklater
Liv Tyler: Star In Ascendance
Blade Runner and the Films of Philip K. Dick
Paul Bowles and Bernardo Bertolucci
Media Hell: Radio, TV and the Press
An Open Letter to the BBC
Detonation Britain: Nuclear War in the UK
Feminism and Shakespeare
Wild Zones: Pornography, Art and Feminism
Sex in Art: Pornography and Pleasure in Painting and Sculpture
Sexing Hardy: Thomas Hardy and Feminism

The Light Eternal is a model monograph, an exemplary job. The subject matter of the book is beautifully
organised and dead on beam. (Lawrence Durrell)
It is amazing for me to see my work treated with such passion and respect. (Andrea Dworkin)

CRESCENT MOON PUBLISHING
P.O. Box 1312, Maidstone, Kent, ME14 5XU, Great Britain. www.crmoon.com

cresmopub@yahoo.co.uk   www.crescentmoon.org.uk

Made in the USA
Middletown, DE
15 July 2022